Perfect Baking With Your
Halogen Oven

Perfect Baking With Your
Halogen Oven

How to create tasty bread, cupcakes, bakes, biscuits and savouries

SARAH FLOWER

A How To Book

ROBINSON

ROBINSON

First published in Great Britain 2011 by Spring Hill
an imprint of How To Books Ltd

This edition published in 2015 by Robinson

A CIP catalogue record for this book
is available from the British Library.

NOTE: The material contained in this book is set out in good faith for general guidance and no
liability can be accepted for loss or expense incurred as a result of relying in particular circumstances
on statements made in the book. Laws and regulations are complex and liable to change, and readers
should check the current position with relevant authorities before making personal arrangements.

ISBN: 978-1-90586-255-9

Produced for How To Books by Deer Park Productions, Tavistock
The halogen oven was supplied courtesy of JML, which can be bought from www.JMLdirect.com
Designed and typeset by Mousemat Design Ltd
Printed and bound in Great Britain by Ashford Colour Press Ltd, Gosport, Hants

Robinson
an imprint of
Little Brown Book Group
Carmelite House
50 Victoria Embankment
London EC4Y 0DZ

An Hachette UK Company
www.hachette.co.uk

www.littlebrown.co.uk

NOTE: The material contained in this book is set out in good faith for general guidance and no
liability can be accepted for loss or expense incurred as a result of relying in particular circumstances
on statements made in the book. Laws and regulations are complex and liable to change, and readers
should check the current position with relevant authorities before making personal arrangements.

How To Books are published by Robinson, an imprint of Little, Brown Book Group.
We welcome proposals from authors who have first-hand experience of their subjects. Please set
out the aims of your book, its target market and its suggested contents in an email to
Nikki.Read@howtobooks.co.uk

There are times when only cake will do. This book is dedicated to my parents, for helping me through some tough times.

Contents

Introduction

I have always loved baking. Ever since I can remember, Sundays were spent baking for the week ahead and this bug has never left me. A huge number of the recipes in this book are family favourites from my mum, aunties and friends – thank you! I have enjoyed rediscovering my childhood through writing this book, though my waistline has definitely suffered! I adore baking; I can be in the worst mood ever but five minutes of baking and I am calm, relaxed and happy. I still have a desire to run my own tea shop – maybe one day!

When I wrote *The Everyday Halogen Oven Cookbook*, it struck me that most halogen oven users dismissed baking and tended to stick to main meals and puddings. I wanted to show readers that you *can* create cakes, biscuits, bread and much more using your halogen. The absolute purist may find that some of the cakes might not turn out exactly as they would if baked in a conventional oven, but the majority are no different and all of them are delightful.

Throughout the book you will find tips on how to make the most of baking in your halogen as well as equipment needed and general advice. If you have purchased any of my previous cookbooks you may find the occasional duplicate recipe. Please excuse this but most recipes require a slightly different technique for cooking in the halogen and I am catering for the newbie halogen user who may not yet be able to adapt their favourite recipe. Don't despair though, there are plenty of new and yummy recipes so you may not even notice the odd duplicate!

I urge bakers to try to use good ingredients as it really does make a difference to certain recipes. I have never made good scones using margarine and budget self-raising flour – much better results come from butter and light self-raising flour. I also use pure extracts, especially for vanilla (I am a big fan of vanilla extract as you may discover in the recipes!). I use Madagascan vanilla extract and vanilla paste. It does cost more than the cheap imitations you can buy from supermarkets but it is well worth the money and does last for ages. I also regularly use pure orange extract and chocolate extract. I also use pastes when using food colouring rather than the cheap liquids you can buy. Pastes create much nicer colours and also don't over wet the icing – so much nicer. You can buy these from cook shops or retailers such as Lakeland or Squires.

The first thing you will realise is that halogen ovens are round and, if you are like me, most of your cake tins will be rectangular – muffin tins are a good example. But don't panic. I use silicon moulds and place them into a round tin. They are perfect and versatile. Don't be tempted to use paper cases as they will not hold their shape and you will end up with flat, wide cupcakes!

I would strongly urge you to purchase an accessory kit and extension ring for your halogen – it will make your life so much easier, believe me! You can buy these from halogen retailers or online from Amazon, Clive James or even eBay.

If you have children, I hope you will involve them in the baking process. Children love cooking and it is great to see them develop a love for food once they are allowed in the kitchen. You can buy some great children's kits, which encourage them to be independent cooks with their own equipment. But be warned: if you are baking cakes with children, once that bowl is ready to be licked, they will grab it and run, so if you want to hold their attention to clean up or decorate avoid giving them the bowl to lick until the last minute! My son gets really annoyed if I use my spatula as it scrapes the bowl clean. Most of the recipes in this book are easy to follow and, with supervision, children should be able to master most – especially those from Chapter 5, Cupcakes, Muffins and Fairy Dust.

I hope you enjoy the book and the results of your baking. Halogen ovens are fantastic machines and, once you have got through the learning process, you should be able to adapt your own recipes.

All the best

Sarah x

Using Your Halogen Oven

As in my first halogen cookbook, this first chapter is dedicated to showing newbie halogen users how to get the most from their machine. So if you have bought both books, you may want to skip this chapter as it contains duplicate information.

Choosing the right machine for you
There are many different halogen ovens on the market, but they are basically all the same machine. The two main variations are the size of bowl and whether the lid is on a hinge. My first machine was from JML when they first started to become popular. I was not really sure what to expect and, over time, it has gained more and more use in our home. Personally I would opt for the largest bowl as this increases the oven's usability. You can also purchase extenders, which can help maximise use. Extenders are metal rings that fit over the top of the halogen bowl, literally extending the height of the bowl and enabling you to fit more into your oven. The lid then fits on top of the extender. They are also useful if you want to keep the food away from the heating elements to prevent burning.

After using the JML, I progressed to the Flavorwave Turbo Platinum Oven. Some of the advantages that this particular oven has over others are that: it has the hinged lid, digital settings, three-speed fan and a pre-heat setting.

Looking at online forums I have noticed that the lids do cause a bit of a bugbear. I had a lid stand beside my JML machine, though annoyingly these are optional extras that you have to purchase and are quite flimsy to look at. Personally, I think it is better to buy the halogen cooker with the hinged lid if you can afford it – this is definitely a safer and easier option.

How do they work?

The halogen oven is a basically a large glass bowl with an electric halogen lid. The lid is heavy as it contains the halogen element, timer and temperature settings. It can be fiddly to clean but I will come to that later. The halogen bulbs heat up the bowl and the fan moves the air around the bowl to create an even temperature. As it is smaller than a conventional oven it heats up faster, reducing the need for long preheating and in some cases reducing the overall cooking time.

This makes it a very popular choice for those watching their pennies, living on their own or, like me, cooking for a busy family. It has even become a popular choice for students and caravanners. I read on a forum that some caravanners use the self-clean facility just like a mini dishwasher – ingenious! It is also popular as a second oven and really becomes invaluable at busy times like Christmas.

For safety, the lid's handle has to be in place (placed securely down) for the machine to turn on. This means that when you lift the lid, the oven is automatically turned off. If you are using the Flavorwave machine with the hinged lid, you have to press the start button to start it and remember to turn the machine off when you lift the lid.

The halogen oven does cook slightly differently to a conventional oven, so first beginning to use it often involves a process of trial and error, but it is not vastly different. If you have favourite recipes that you cook in the conventional oven, try them in the halogen. I find cooking at a slightly lower temperature or cooking for less time normally gives the same results, but hopefully this book will help give you more confidence.

The halogen oven is not a microwave and does not work in the same way as a microwave, so if you are thinking you can cook food in minutes you are wrong. It does, however, have a multitude of functions – defrosting, baking, grilling, roasting and steaming are all perfect for the halogen. Remember that to get the optimum benefit air needs to circulate around the bowl, so ideally place dishes and trays on racks and avoid the temptation to over fill.

Getting the right equipment
This sounds obvious but … make sure you have oven trays, baking sheets and casserole dishes that will fit inside the halogen oven. There is nothing more frustrating than planning a meal and just at the last minute realising that your dish does not fit in the machine! You can use any ovenproof dish or tray – metal, silicon and Pyrex are all fine. The halogen oven is round so it makes sense to look at trays and stands of the same shape, just smaller so you can remove them without burning yourself!

When I first started using the halogen, it was frustrating to find that 80% of my bakeware did not fit in the machine, but a quick revamp and purchase of the accessories have proved invaluable. If money is tight, you can find great casserole dishes at boot sales or charity shops – you don't have to spend a fortune on new cookware.

You can also buy an accessories pack, which contains steamer pans, grilling pans, toasting racks and even an extension ring. These are highly recommended if you use your oven regularly and certainly enhance what you can do with the machine. There are many websites selling or advertising these accessories, so a general internet search will point you in the right direction. Amazon is also a great place to look.

Let there be light

As experienced halogen users will know, the halogen light turns on and off during cooking. This is not a fault of the thermostat as some people have mentioned on forums. It literally turns off when the programmed temperature is reached, then on again when it drops. Set the temperature and marvel at how quickly the oven reaches the required temperature – literally in minutes. I love the light – along with being able to watch your food cook, there is something quite cosy about walking into your kitchen on a winter or autumn evening and seeing the glow of the halogen cooker.

Timings

The halogen oven comes with a 60-minute timer and temperature setting dials. The Flavorwave Turbo also comes with three fan settings and a digital timer. All halogens turn off when the timer settings have been reached. This means you can be reassured that if the phone rings or you are called away from the kitchen, your food won't spoil.

Size

The oven is small enough to sit on a worktop, but do allow space for removal of the lid if it is not hinged. The lid can get very hot and is quite large and heavy, being the brains of the machine, so it can be a good idea to buy the lid stand. However, be careful when using this stand as it can seem quite flimsy until you get used to it. You could opt to place the lid on a heatproof surface but, again, be careful not to burn yourself or your worktop!

Careful does it

Your oven should come with some tong type of gadget to help you lift out the racks. They are quite useful, but I also use a more substantial set of tongs. As with any oven or cooker, do be careful as the bowl and contents get very hot. I find using proper oven gloves a necessity as they cover your whole hand and wrist and can prevent accidents.

As with all electrical and hot appliances, do not let your children near the halogen – the glass bowl gets very hot.

Foil and coverings

Some people like to use foil when cooking. This can be a good idea as it prevents food from browning too quickly or it can be used to parcel foods, but make sure the foil is secure. The fan is very strong and if the foil is not secure it could float around the oven and might damage the element. Another option for preventing burning is obviously to turn the temperature down or place the food further away from the element (use the low rack or add an extension ring).

Cleaning your oven

The halogen is promoted as being self-cleaning. This basically means that you fill it with a little water and a squirt of washing-up liquid and then turn it on to the wash setting. The combination of the fan and the heat allows the water to swish around the bowl giving it a quick clean. This normally takes about 10 minutes. Personally, I find it just as simple to remove the bowl and place it in the dishwasher – it always comes out gleaming.

The lid is a little more difficult to clean and I would refer to the manufacturer's guidelines as each product can be a little different. Do not get the element or electrical parts wet!

High and low racks
There are two standard racks which come with every halogen oven – a high and a low rack. The high rack is placed nearer the element so use this if you want to brown something. The low rack is used more for longer cooking times.

You can also cook directly on the bottom of the bowl. I do this quite often, particularly if I am being lazy and just want to chuck in some oven chips. It does cook well but takes a little longer compared to using the racks, as air is not able to circulate all around the food.

Baking
Some people worry about using the halogen to bake cakes but I think this is because they are setting the oven temperature too high, resulting in a crusty brown cake top with a soggy middle. Setting the oven to a lower temperature can solve this problem. Muffins and cupcakes take between 12 and 18 minutes. You only really encounter problems with cakes if you are cooking for too long at too high a temperature. Try some of my cake recipes and you will see how simple it can be.

Preheat or not to preheat
Most recipes I have found on forums don't mention preheating the oven. This is probably due to the speed the oven takes to reach its temperature setting. However, I think it is worth turning the oven on 2 minutes before use

just to bring it up to the right temperature.

I found this to be the case when attempting to cook soft-boiled eggs. According to the Flavorwave recipe book, I should be able to cook a soft egg in 6 minutes just by placing it on the high rack. It didn't work, but when I tried again in a heated oven it was much more successful.

Some machines (such as the Flavorwave) have a preheat button which preheats at 260°C for 6 minutes, but others, such as the JML, require you to set to the required temperature and turn on.

Weights and measures

I am constantly being asked for the recipes for my cakes and it always throws me into turmoil as I never measure anything when baking. My husband laughs as he sees me literally throwing in all sorts of ingredients, seemingly oblivious to the end result. Thankfully they all come out perfectly yummy! Don't follow my lead – until you are confident, measure as you go. There is some great measuring equipment available to make life easier.

Measuring spoons

You can buy a neat little set of measuring spoons for around £2. They are ideal for recipes that need teaspoon, tablespoon or dessertspoon measurements.

Measuring cups

These are good for measuring dry ingredients or liquids. Some show measures for key ingredients such as flour or sugar, others just measure in millilitres.

Measuring jug

I use a glass Pyrex measuring jug. They are very hardy and come up gleaming after every wash – unlike plastic jugs which can stain. Measuring jugs are ideal for measuring liquids or mixing ingredients together. I also have a great Pyrex measuring jug which shows grammes for sugar, flour and mixed fruit. I have picked up various pieces of kitchenalia from boot sales and auctions over the years.

Scales

Find a set of scales that suits your kitchen. I like the retro-looking scales with a deep bowl, which is ideal for weighing a variety of ingredients. Scales can cost as little as £3 to buy new.

Weights table

1 ounce is equal to approximately 28g, but for ease of use, most tables round down to 25g per ounce and gradually increase this as the weight increases. See the table below for clarity.

I hope this chapter has not confused you. Move on to try some recipes and then come back to this chapter at a later date – it will probably make more sense then!

Enjoy!

WEIGHT	
Metric (approx.)	Imperial
25–30g	1oz
50–55g	2oz
85g	3oz
100g	3.5oz
125g	4oz
150g	5oz
175g	6oz
200g	7oz
225g	8oz
250g	9oz
280g	10oz
350g	12oz
400g	14oz
450g	16oz/1lb
900kg	2lb

LIQUID MEASURE	
Metric (approx.)	Imperial
5ml	1 teaspoon (tsp)
15ml	1 tablespoon (tbsp)
25–30ml	1 fl oz
50ml	2 fl oz
75ml	3 fl oz
100–125ml	4 fl oz
150ml	5 fl oz
175ml	6 fl oz
200ml	7 fl oz
225ml	8 fl oz
250ml	9 fl oz
300ml	10 fl oz (½ pint)
600ml	20 fl oz (1 pint)
1 litre	1¾ pints

Top Baking Tips

Here is a collection of tips that I hope will help save you time or enhance your baking experience.

Read!

Always read the recipe right through before you start. Not only does this familiarise you with what you have to do, but it also gives you time to check your ingredients and equipment and prepare your timings. There is no point starting a recipe, only to get to the middle bit and find out that you have to soak something overnight before you proceed to the next step – I know, I have been that idiot!

Preparing your cake tins

I cannot emphasise enough the importance of lining or greasing your cake tins thoroughly before baking. I am a recent convert to cake tin liners. You can buy them for very little from your local supermarket or cake store and they are well worth the investment. You can also buy reusable baking sheets – these are great but remember that most will be made to fit conventional ovens so you will have to make adjustments or seek alternatives for your halogen.

If you want to line the tins yourself, you can butter the tin and then sprinkle with a coating of flour to make it non-stick. Alternatively, use baking parchment cut to size, though this will also have to be placed into a buttered tin.

Cooling racks

It is really important to cool cakes, biscuits or breads on a cooling rack, allowing the air to circulate all around. Cooling racks (also known as wire racks) are relatively cheap to buy but, if you don't have one, you could use the grill rack off your grill tray. Most cakes need to cool for up to 5 minutes in the tin before you turn them out onto the rack.

Mixing

Don't over or under mix – I know this sounds difficult, but you will get used to it. Creaming the butter and sugar until light and fluffy takes only a minute or two in a food mixer. I personally still fold in the flour but that is just force of habit, although over mixing the flour can give tougher results. One good example of being careful not to over mix is when thickening double cream. Stop when it reaches the consistency of light peaks, as once over whipped it will go lumpy and horrible.

Pastry

Pastry loves to be cold. Use cold butter (or even frozen – see Chapter 8, Tart It Up and Roll It Out). I always leave my dough in the fridge for at least 10 minutes before using – not only does this keep the pastry cool, it also helps avoid shrinkage when rolling out or baking as this time has allowed the pastry to relax. Don't handle the dough too much – a food processor makes light work of pastry.

Cake making tips

You may follow a recipe exactly but your cake decides not to come out exactly like the celebrity chef's – why does this happen? Well, with cake baking there are so many things that can affect the end result, even simple changes in temperature or your own frame of mind. Here are some basic tips to help.

- **A doughy cake** – often caused by too little raising agent, unsifted flour or not baking for long enough or at the right temperature to allow the cake to rise.
- **A heavy cake** – may be caused by not mixing correctly (adding enough air to the mixture), not sifting the flour, not using enough raising agent or using too much flour.
- **A dry cake** – tends to be overcooked or perhaps not enough butter or wet ingredients were used. If this occurs frequently, check your timings. If your fruit cakes are dry, try grating a carrot, apple or even a mashed banana into the mixture as this will help to moisten the cake.
- **Fruit sunk to the bottom of the cake** – mainly caused by adding the fruit before the main sponge cake is mixed (i.e. you should cream the butter and sugar, add the beaten eggs and then the sifted flour, before adding the fruit mixture). You may not have combined the fruit well enough, or simply made the cake mix too thin so it could not hold the additional ingredients.
- **Sunken cakes** – normally caused by those impatient souls who can't resist opening the oven door every few minutes 'just to check'. That's what glass doors are for! You may also have had too much liquid in your cake mix.
- **Burnt top, uncooked middle** – your oven temperature

is too hot. Turn the temperature down and cook for longer. Ignore those friendly tips about using tin foil in order to convince the cake to cook quicker – you will not get the right results. Remember you can't rush perfection!

- **Cracked top** – your oven is too hot. Turn the temperature down and cook for a little longer. An uneven surface (one side risen and the other low) can indicate uneven temperature.

- **Preheat your oven** – I know the halogen appears not to require this, but old habits die hard. I prefer to preheat and know that when my cake enters the oven, it starts cooking immediately and does not get confused by rising temperatures.

Cookies and biscuits

Don't over mix cookies or biscuits as this could give tough results. Also remember that biscuits and cookies harden once cooled, so avoid overcooking unless you want to break your teeth on them!

Butter icing

When mixing icing sugar, you may end up in a white cloud of dust if you are not careful. Don't be over zealous with the icing sugar at first. Add a little at a time – yes it may take longer, but you will avoid the dust cloud and remain in control.

Chocolate

When melting chocolate, use a bain marie or place a heatproof bowl over a pan of boiling water. Be careful not to let the water touch the bottom of the bowl as this will result in thick and unusable chocolate. When a recipe asks for chocolate, try to use the best quality you can. Some cheap cooking chocolate is far removed from the real thing – sweet and not really that nice. I prefer to use dark chocolate with at least 70% cocoa content. I also buy as a special treat (and it lasts for ages) Willie Harcourt's Pure Cacao (£5.99 from Waitrose or visit www.williescacao.com) for some great savoury and sweet recipes. I am a huge fan, even more so as it is actually a very healthy product … chocolate and healthy – my type of food!

Lemons and limes
You may be familiar with this scenario – you need the juice of a lemon or lime, but it just seems so difficult to squeeze out the juice. Top tip: warm the lemon or lime gently. Once warm, they will release their juice with ease.

Finish with style
You have made a cake or dish that tastes wonderful but maybe lacks kerb appeal – well, learn to finish with style! Sprinkle icing sugar or sift cocoa over the top of a cake, spread with butter icing or top with fresh fruit. A glaze of dried fruit and nuts tastefully covers the top of a fruit cake, or even grab some fondant icing and let your inner child free to create (remember play-dough!).

Don't despair if things go a bit awry when you first start baking. It is a learning process and, remember, tasty cakes come in all shapes and sizes and if you are baking for your children, they simply won't care – 'just give me the cake!'

Tasty Savouries

'One of the very nicest things about life is the way we must regularly stop whatever it is we are doing and devote our attention to eating.'
– Luciano Pavarotti and William Wright, *Pavarotti, My Own Story*

Whether you are catering for a packed lunch, picnic or afternoon tea, savoury snacks are essential. Here is a selection of recipes that can, mostly, be eaten hot or cold, as a snack or a main meal. Enjoy!

Cheese Scones

MAKES 8–10

200g self-raising flour
1 teaspoon mustard
   powder
Pinch of cayenne
   pepper
Seasoning to taste
30g butter
60g mature Cheddar,
   grated
125ml milk

SUITABLE FOR VEGETARIANS

- Preheat the halogen oven using the preheat setting or set the temperature to 210°C.
- Sift the flour into a bowl. Add the mustard and cayenne pepper, and season to taste.
- Add the butter and rub to form breadcrumbs. Add the grated cheese and combine well.
- Gradually add the milk and mix to form a firm but not wet dough.
- Place the dough on a floured board and press out to a 3–4cm thickness. Cut with a pastry cutter and place on a greased baking tray. Brush with milk or egg.
- Place in the halogen oven for 10–15 minutes. Don't overcook – I was always told that scones should look a bit pale when cooked. Remove them from the oven when they are only slightly golden – too brown and they will be hard and dry once cool.
- Place on a cooling rack or serve warm!

Note: You can also use this recipe to form a cobbler topping on a savoury dish.

Cheese and Onion Scones

MAKES 8–10

- In a frying or sauté pan, add the chopped onion and cook until golden – ideally so it is a little brown, almost caramelised. Once cooked, leave to one side.
- Preheat the halogen oven using the preheat setting or set the temperature to 210°C.
- Sift the flour into a bowl. Add the cayenne and mustard and season to taste.
- Add the butter and rub to form breadcrumbs. Add the grated cheddar and parmesan. Combine well.
- Gradually add the milk and mix to form a dough that is firm but not wet.
- Place this dough on a floured board, and press out to a 3–4cm thickness. Cut with a pastry cutter and place on a greased baking tray. Brush with milk or egg.
- Place in the halogen oven for 10–15 minutes. Don't overcook. Remove them from the oven when they are only slightly golden – too brown and they will be hard and dry once cool.
- Place on a cooling rack or serve warm!

Note: Try adding some chopped cooked bacon or pancetta for a delicious savoury scone. Experiment by adding your favourite herbs. You can also use this recipe to form a cobbler topping on a savoury dish.

1 onion, finely chopped
200g self-raising flour
Pinch of cayenne pepper
1 teaspoon mustard powder
Seasoning to taste
30g butter
60g mature Cheddar, grated
25g parmesan, grated
125ml milk

SUITABLE FOR VEGETARIANS

Goat's Cheese and Sundried Tomato Scones

Makes 8–10

200g self-raising flour
Seasoning
30g butter
60g goat's cheese,
   crumbled
6–8 sundried tomatoes
   in oil, drained and
   finely chopped
100–125ml milk

SUITABLE FOR VEGETARIANS

- Preheat the halogen oven using the preheat setting or set the temperature to 210°C.
- Sift the flour into a bowl. Season to taste.
- Add the butter and rub to form breadcrumbs. Add the crumbled goat's cheese and sundried tomatoes and combine well.
- Gradually add the milk a little at a time, mixing until you form a dough which should be firm but not wet.
- Place the dough on a floured board, and press out to a 3–4cm thickness. Cut with a pastry cutter and place on a greased baking tray. Brush with milk or egg.
- Place in the halogen oven for 10–15 minutes. Don't overcook – I was always told that scones should look a bit pale when cooked. Remove them from the oven when they are only slightly golden – too brown and they will be hard and dry once cool.
- Place on a cooling rack or serve warm!

Tomato and Mozzarella Puff Tarts

Puff pastry is the busy cook's best friend. You can create your own toppings but this is a simple favourite to help get you started.

- Roll out the pastry to a 2–3mm thickness. Cut into 4–6 squares. Carefully score around each square, 1cm from the edge – do not cut the pastry, just make a slight indent.
- Preheat the halogen oven using the preheat setting or turn on to 210°C.
- In the middle of each square add a teaspoon of sundried tomato paste and spread evenly within the scored line. Place pieces of mozzarella and a few basil leaves inside the scored line. Add a few cherry tomatoes, halved or whole, depending on your preference. Season to taste.
- Place on the high rack and bake for about 15 minutes until the pastry is golden. If the tarts start to brown before the base is cooked, transfer to the low rack for a few more minutes.
- Before serving, add a garnish of basil leaves.

SERVES 4

½ pack readymade puff pastry
4 teaspoons sundried tomato paste
1 pack mozzarella
Handful of basil leaves
8–10 cherry tomatoes
Seasoning to taste

SUITABLE FOR VEGETARIANS

MAKES 10–14

225g bread flour
1 teaspoon paprika
½ teaspoon salt
Black pepper to taste
7g dried yeast
30g butter
1 large egg, beaten
125ml warm milk
Drizzle of olive oil
1 large onion, finely
   chopped
6–8 rashers bacon or
   pancetta
75g mature Cheddar,
   grated
1 teaspoon dried
   oregano

This recipe is a variation on the popular Chelsea Buns. We used to make these when we were children and I always loved them. They are easy to make.

Savoury Wheels

- In a large bowl, add the flour, paprika, salt, pepper and dried yeast. Combine well.
- Rub in the butter to form a texture similar to breadcrumbs. Once combined, add the egg and warm milk. Combine well to form a dough.
- On a floured surface, knead the dough for 5 minutes. Place it back in the bowl, cover and keep in a warm place for 30–40 minutes or until it has doubled in size.
- Meanwhile, heat the oil in a sauté pan. Add the chopped onion and bacon pieces. Cook until the onion is soft and the bacon is starting to go crispy. Remove and leave to one side.
- Preheat the halogen oven using the preheat setting or set the temperature to 180°C.
- When the dough is ready, place it back on the floured surface and knead again for another 5 minutes. Then roll it into a large rectangle of roughly 30cm, making sure there are no breaks in the dough.
- Leaving a gap of approximately 2cm around the edge, cover the dough evenly with the bacon and onion. Finish with grated cheese and a sprinkle of oregano. Season to taste.
- Holding the end of the dough nearest to you, gently lift and roll to create a large sausage.
- Using a sharp serrated knife, cut 2cm slices. Place these on a well-greased or lined baking tray.
- Place in the halogen oven on the low rack.
- Cook for 20–25 minutes until golden and risen. If the undersides are not done to perfection, turn them over and cook for another 5 minutes.
- Serve hot or cold.

Sundried Tomato, Mozzarella and Basil Wheels

MAKES 10–14

- In a large bowl, add the flour, paprika, salt, pepper and dried yeast. Combine well.
- Rub in the butter to form a texture similar to breadcrumbs. Once combined, add the egg and warm milk. Combine well to form a dough.
- On a floured surface, knead the dough for 5 minutes. Return it to the bowl, cover and keep in a warm place for 30–40 minutes or until it has doubled in size.
- Preheat the halogen oven using the preheat setting or set the temperature to 180°C.
- When the dough is ready, place it back on the floured surface and knead again for another 5 minutes.
- Roll into a large rectangle, roughly 30cm, making sure there are no breaks in the dough.
- Leaving a gap of approximately 2cm around the edge, cover the dough with occasional, but evenly distributed, dollops of pesto. Top this with the sundried tomatoes, torn mozzarella and basil leaves. Season to taste.
- Holding the end of the dough nearest to you, gently lift and roll to create a large sausage.
- Using a sharp serrated knife, cut 2cm slices. Place these on a well greased or lined baking tray.
- Place in the halogen oven on the low rack.
- Cook for 20–25 minutes until golden and risen. If you find the bottoms are not done as well as you would like, turn them over and cook for another 5 minutes.
- Serve hot or cold.

225g bread flour
1 teaspoon paprika
½ teaspoon salt
Black pepper to taste
7g dried yeast
30g butter
1 large egg, beaten
125ml warm milk
2–3 teaspoons sundried tomato pesto
15–20 sundried tomatoes (in oil)
1 large ball of mozzarella, torn
Handful of fresh basil

SUITABLE FOR VEGETARIANS

SERVES 4

5 eggs
1 bunch spring
onions, finely
chopped
500g cooked potatoes,
sliced or cubed
50–75g mature cheese
1 teaspoon thyme
(optional)
Seasoning to taste

SUITABLE FOR VEGETARIANS

Potato, Cheese and Spring Onion Tortilla

This is an ideal dish for using up any leftover cooked potatoes.

- Preheat the halogen oven using the preheat setting or set the temperature to 200°C.
- In a large bowl, add the eggs and beat well. Add the remaining ingredients and combine. Pour into a well-greased ovenproof dish.
- Place on the low rack and cook for 20–25 minutes until it is firm.
- Serve hot or cold with salad.

Mediterranean-style Tortilla

This is an ideal dish for using up any leftover vegetables – anything goes, so experiment!

- Preheat the halogen oven using the preheat setting or set the temperature to 200°C.
- In a large bowl, add the eggs and beat well. Add the remaining ingredients and combine.
- Pour this into a well-greased ovenproof dish.
- Place on the low rack and cook for 20–25 minutes until it is firm.
- Serve hot or cold with salad.

SERVES 4

5 eggs
1 bunch spring onions, finely chopped
1–2 red peppers, diced or thinly sliced
6 rashers pancetta, diced
3–4 sundried tomatoes, chopped
50g parmesan, grated
Small handful of fresh herbs (basil, oregano or thyme would suit)
Seasoning to taste

Savoury Potato Balls

4–5 potatoes, cooked
30g red Leicester
  cheese, grated
40g mature Cheddar,
  grated
1 tablespoon butter
1 small onion, very
  finely chopped
1 tablespoon parsley,
  finely chopped
½ tablespoon thyme,
  chopped
Black pepper
Sea salt
50g sesame seeds

SUITABLE FOR VEGETARIANS

I discovered this recipe in an old notebook that used to belong to my neighbour. I tried them out and they are fabulous. I hope you enjoy them! I used a combination of red Leicester and mature cheddar but you can opt for whatever you prefer – parmesan, mozzarella and even goat's cheese would work. You can also add some chopped chillies for a nice hit. I like to dip these potato balls in a rich chilli sauce so I tend not to add chillies to my recipe.

• You need to use cooked potatoes for this recipe, but cold potatoes don't have the same loveliness when they are mashed as warm potatoes. For this reason, I heat them gently just prior to using. This is entirely up to you but I find it is nicer.
• Mash the potatoes and add the grated cheese, butter, finely chopped onion, herbs and seasoning. Combine well.
• Roll into small balls and then roll onto a saucer of sesame seeds before placing on a greased baking tray.
• Preheat the halogen oven using the preheat setting or set the temperature to 175°C.
• Place on the low rack and cook for 15 minutes until golden.
• Serve hot or cold.

Quiche Lorraine

When making tarts, quiches or pies, I find it is much better to bake the pastry case first as this can prevent the horrible soggy bottom scenario. Personally I prefer using wholemeal or wholegrain flour to make a savoury pastry, but this is entirely your choice.

100g plain flour
50g cold butter
200ml milk
3 eggs
1 teaspoon mustard
    powder
1 teaspoon cornflour
Pinch of cayenne
    pepper
150g Gruyère cheese,
    grated
1 small onion, finely
    chopped
75g cooked ham or
    lean bacon, diced
Seasoning to taste

- Make the pastry. Place the flour in a large bowl and add small pieces of the chilled butter. Using your fingertips, rub the butter into the flour until the whole mix resembles breadcrumbs. Add 5–6 tablespoons of cold water (a little at a time) and mix until it forms a dough. Wrap the dough in cling film and place in the fridge to cool until needed.
- Preheat the halogen oven using the preheat setting or set the temperature to 200°C.
- Roll out the pastry on a floured surface to the correct size and thickness to line a 23cm greased flan tin. Place a sheet of baking parchment over the pastry and cover with baking beans.
- Bake on the low rack for 10 minutes. Remove the baking beans and parchment and cook for a further 5 minutes. Remove the pastry case from the oven and turn the oven down to 190°C.
- Meanwhile, mix the milk and eggs together thoroughly before adding the mustard powder, cornflour and a pinch of cayenne pepper. Add the cheese, onion and bacon or ham. Season well before pouring into the pastry case.
- Bake on the low rack 30–45 minutes until golden and the centre is firm. If the top starts to get too dark, cover with tin foil, making sure it is secure.

SERVES 4–6

40g butter
6 sheets filo pastry
400g baby leaf
   spinach, roughly
   torn
250g feta cheese,
   crumbled
¼ teaspoon nutmeg
Seasoning
Sesame seeds

SUITABLE FOR VEGETARIANS

Spinach and Feta Pie

Serve this with a selection of fresh salad dishes and new potatoes – the perfect dish for a summer's evening.

- Preheat the halogen oven using the preheat setting or set the temperature to 200°C.
- Melt the butter in a saucepan or place it in a bowl in your halogen oven to melt, though make sure it does not burn.
- Layer 3 sheets of pastry in the base of a pie dish (make sure the dish fits comfortably within your halogen). Brush butter between the sheets and allow them to hang over the edge to give you enough to form the sides of the pie.
- Place a thin layer of spinach leaves, then a layer of crumbled feta and a little nutmeg and season with black pepper. Repeat this, finishing with the feta layer.
- Cover with more filo sheets, again brushing with butter. Bring the edges together to form a crust and remove any excess pastry.
- Brush with butter and sprinkle with sesame seeds.
- Place on the low rack and bake for 30–40 minutes, until golden.

Traditional Cornish Pasties

SERVES 4–6

As I live on the Cornish border, it seems appropriate to include a traditional Cornish staple.

- Make the pastry. Place the flour in a large bowl and add small pieces of the chilled butter. Using your fingertips, rub the butter into the flour until the whole mix resembles breadcrumbs. Add 2–4 tablespoons of cold water (a little at a time) and mix until it forms a dough. Wrap the dough in cling film and place in the fridge to cool until needed.
- Chop the vegetables and steak into small dice-sized pieces. Place in a bowl and mix thoroughly. Add the paprika and herbs and season well.
- Roll out the pastry on a floured surface until even. Using a small round plate approximately 20cm in diameter as a template, cut 4 circles.
- Preheat the halogen oven using the preheat setting or set the oven temperature to 210°C.
- Place some of the steak and vegetable mix in the centre of each circle – do not overfill. Use beaten egg or water to brush the edges of the pastry before bringing them together and crimping until sealed.
- Place the pasties on a lined baking tray. Brush with beaten egg.
- Place on the lower rack and bake for 20 minutes until the pastry starts to turn golden. Reduce the heat to 150°C and cook for a further 20–25 minutes. If the bottoms of the pasties are not cooked to your liking, turn them over for the last 5–10 minutes of cooking.
- Remove from the oven immediately and place on a cooling rack.

150g plain flour
75g cold butter
1 onion
1 carrot
1 potato
100g swede
350g lean rump steak
1 teaspoon paprika
1 teaspoon mixed
  herbs (optional)
Seasoning to taste
1 egg, beaten

Sundried Tomato and Goat's Cheese Frittata

SERVES 4–6

5 eggs

4–5 spring onions,
  finely chopped

110g goat's cheese,
  crumbled

4–6 sundried
  tomatoes, chopped

1 teaspoon mixed
  herbs

Seasoning to taste

SUITABLE FOR VEGETARIANS

- Preheat the halogen oven using the preheat setting or set the temperature to 200°C.
- In a large bowl, add the eggs and beat well. Add the remaining ingredients and combine.
- Pour this into a well greased ovenproof dish.
- Place on the low rack and cook for 20–25 minutes until it is firm.
- Serve hot or cold with salad.

Corned Beef and Potato Tart

SERVES 4

I prefer to bake the pastry case before adding the corned beef and potato mixture.

- Make the pastry. Place the flour in a large bowl and add small pieces of the chilled butter. Using your fingertips, rub the butter into the flour until the whole mix resembles breadcrumbs. Add 2–3 tablespoons of cold water (a little at a time) and mix until it forms a dough. Wrap the dough in cling film and place in the fridge to cool until needed.
- Cook and mash the potatoes.
- Place the corned beef, mashed potato and diced onion in a bowl and mix thoroughly. Add the Worcestershire sauce and beaten egg and season well.
- Preheat the halogen oven using the preheat setting or set to 200°C.
- Roll out the pastry on a floured surface until even. Line the pie dish with the pastry and trim. Place a piece of baking parchment over the pastry, cover with baking beans and cook on the low rack for 10 minutes (i.e. blind bake).
- Remove the baking beans and parchment and add the corned beef mix.
- Place back on the low rack and bake for 25–35 minutes until golden.
- Serve sliced, hot or cold.

100g plain flour
50g cold butter
3–4 potatoes, cooked and mashed (you can use leftover mash for this)
350g or 1 tin corned beef
1 onion, diced
1–2 teaspoons Worcestershire sauce
1 egg, beaten
Seasoning to taste

Tofu and Stilton Quiche

SERVES 4–6

100g plain flour
50g cold butter
1 box tofu, mashed
125g mature Cheddar, grated (you can use vegan Cheddar if you want a vegan quiche)
1 onion, finely chopped
1 tablespoon Marigold Nutritional Yeast Flakes (optional but gives a cheesier taste and is full of B vitamins)
Dash of milk (optional)
Seasoning to taste
40–50g Stilton or blue cheese

SUITABLE FOR VEGETARIANS

- Make the pastry. Place the flour in a large bowl and add small pieces of the chilled butter. Using your fingertips, rub the butter into the flour until the whole mix resembles breadcrumbs. Add 2–3 tablespoons of cold water (a little at a time) and mix until it forms a dough. Wrap the dough in cling film and place in the fridge to cool until needed.
- Preheat the halogen oven using the preheat setting or set the temperature to 200°C.
- Roll out the pastry on a floured surface to the correct size and thickness to line a 23cm greased flan tin. Place a sheet of baking parchment over the pastry and cover with baking beans. Bake for 10 minutes.
- Remove the baking beans and parchment and cook for a further 5 minutes. Then remove the pastry case from the oven and turn the oven down to 180°C.
- Meanwhile, mash the tofu thoroughly. Add the grated Cheddar, onion and nutritional yeast flakes if using. If the mixture is too dry, add a dash of milk and mix well. Don't make the mixture too wet.
- Season well before pouring into the pastry case. Cover with a sprinkling of crumbled Stilton before placing on the high rack.
- Bake for 20–30 minutes until golden. Remove from the oven immediately once cooked to prevent the base of the pastry going soggy with the condensation of the oven.

Stuffed Tomatoes

Perfect for a summer's evening with minted new potatoes and various salad dishes – I can almost smell the freshly mowed grass!

- Preheat the halogen oven using the preheat setting or turn the temperature to 180°C.
- Carefully cut off the tops of the tomatoes and scoop out the flesh. Chop the discarded tops finely and place in a bowl along with the flesh. Place the tomatoes on a baking tray and leave to one side until needed.
- In a sauté pan, fry the onion and garlic in olive oil for a couple of minutes before adding the red pepper. Cook until soft.
- Remove from the heat and add to the bowl of tomato flesh. Add the pine nuts and basil leaves.
- Re-hydrate the couscous following the instructions on the pack. Once re-hydrated, add it to the bowl. Season to taste and stir well to combine all the ingredients.
- Spoon this mixture into the tomatoes, finishing with some crumbled mozzarella. Grind some black pepper over the top before placing on the low rack and cooking for 25–30 minutes.

SERVES 4–6

4–6 beefsteak tomatoes
Drizzle of olive oil
1 red onion, finely chopped
2–3 cloves of garlic, crushed
½ red pepper
20g pine nuts
Small handful of basil leaves, chopped
50–75g couscous, re-hydrated with a little hot water
40g mozzarella, crumbled
Seasoning to taste

SUITABLE FOR VEGETARIANS

Cheating Cheesy Straws

1 packet puff pastry
100g mature Cheddar
Handful of dried
   onions
Sprinkle of chives,
   freshly chopped
   (optional)

I am a big fan of the TV
chefs The Hairy Bikers
and saw them use this on
their BBC show. It is a
great idea and creates
light straws with little
effort.

SUITABLE FOR VEGETARIANS

- Roll out the puff pastry to the same thickness as if you were making a pie.
- Sprinkle with some of the Cheddar, onions and chives and carefully fold in half.
- Sprinkle again with Cheddar, onions and chives and fold again. If possible, do this once more.
- Carefully roll out the pastry again to the same thickness as if making a pie. If the filling falls out, just place it back in the pastry.
- Once rolled, cut into thin strips. You can give these strips a little twist before placing onto a lined baking tray.
- Bake in the oven at 210°C on the high rack for 15 minutes until golden. Leave on the tray for 5 minutes before transferring to a cooling rack.

Variations:
- **Bacon & Cheese Straws** – add bacon or pancetta for added flavour.
- **Marmite Straws** – spread each fold with yeast extract for lovers of Marmite.
- **Chilli Straws** – add a sprinkle of paprika and chilli powder to each layer. For added kick, sprinkle with a few finely chopped chillis.
- **Garlic Butter Straws** – mix some butter, crushed garlic and mixed herbs together. Spread thinly over each layer.
- **Chocolate Straws** – chocolate lovers: try spreading each fold with chocolate spread or sprinkles of dark chocolate chips.
- **Cinnamon Straws** – fill folds with a generous sprinkling of cinnamon and mixed dried fruit (sultanas or raisins).

Or why not create some of your own!

Spicy Go Nuts and Seeds

- Preheat the halogen oven using the preheat setting or set the temperature to 150°C.
- Crush the coriander and fenugreek seeds and combine well with the other spices.
- Place the nuts and seeds in a bowl and combine.
- On your hob, heat the olive oil and add the spices. Combine well and cook for 1–2 minutes to help release the flavours. Pour this onto the nuts and seeds and combine well.
- Pour the nuts and seeds onto a baking tray and place on the low rack for 20 minutes, shaking and turning halfway through the cooking time.
- Place back in the bowl and sprinkle with zatar and sea salt. Combine well. Leave to cool before storing in airtight container.

1 teaspoon coriander seeds
1 teaspoon cracked fenugreek seeds
1 teaspoon paprika
1 teaspoon cumin
1–2 teaspoons chilli powder
Black pepper to taste
½ teaspoon garlic salt
350g mixed small nuts and seeds
1–2 tablespoons olive oil
Sprinkle of zatar (thyme and sesame seasoning mix)
Sprinkle of sea salt

SUITABLE FOR VEGETARIANS

Cheese and Onion Tarts

SERVES 4-6

100g wholemeal,
   granary or plain
   flour
50g butter
1 large onion, finely
   chopped
75g cream cheese
150g mature cheddar,
   grated
½ teaspoon wholegrain
   mustard
Seasoning to taste

SUITABLE FOR VEGETARIANS

These are perfect for a packed lunch or picnic.

• Place the flour in a bowl and rub in the butter to
  form breadcrumbs. Add a little water until you have
  made a firm dough. Place in the fridge to chill for 5
  minutes.
• Roll out the pastry to the desired thickness and line
  4–6 small tartlet tins.
• Preheat the halogen oven using the preheat setting or
  set the temperature to 200°C.
• Place the tartlets on the low rack and cook for 10
  minutes (ie baking blind).
• Meanwhile, heat a pan with a little olive oil and add
  the chopped onion. Cook until soft and remove.
• In a bowl mix the onion, cream cheese, grated
  mature cheese, wholegrain mustard and season to
  taste.
• Place this mixture in the tartlet cases and place on
  the high rack. Cook for 15–20 minutes until golden
  and firm.
• Serve hot or cold.

Cheesy Sausage Rolls

MAKES 12–18

This is a lovely recipe and perfect for picnics or packed lunches. I use cooked cocktail sausages but you can choose your own filling. Vegetarians can opt for veggie sausages cut in half or Sosmix.

350g self-raising flour
Pinch of sea salt
1 teaspoon paprika
Pinch of cayenne pepper (optional)
Black pepper to season
50g mature Cheddar, grated
225ml milk
45ml vegetable oil
1 egg
12–18 cocktail sausages
Egg or milk to glaze
Sprinkle of sesame seeds

- Sift the flour into a bowl and add the salt, paprika and cayenne pepper. Season with black pepper. Stir in the grated cheese.
- In a jug, add the milk, oil and egg and beat until combined. Pour this onto the flour and mix to form a dough. The dough needs to be soft but not so sticky that it sticks to the surface. Add more flour if necessary.
- Place on a floured surface and roll to a thickness of about 4–5mm. Cut into rectangles large enough to roll the sausages in.
- Roll up the sausages in the dough and place seam-side down on a greased browning tray. Glaze with egg or milk and a sprinkle of sesame seeds.
- Preheat the halogen oven using the preheat setting or set the temperature to 210°C.
- Place the sausage rolls on the high rack and cook for 15 minutes until golden. Check the undersides of the rolls to see if they are browned enough (I use the browning tray as it helps to brown them). If they are not done to your satisfaction, carefully turn them over and cook for another couple of minutes.
- Serve hot or cold.

350g self-raising flour
Pinch of sea salt
1 teaspoon paprika
Pinch of cayenne
  pepper
Black pepper to
  season
1–2 chillies, finely
  chopped
25g mature Cheddar,
  grated (optional)
225ml milk
45ml vegetable oil
Dash of Tabasco sauce
1 egg
12–18 cocktail
  sausages
Egg or milk to glaze
Sesame seeds

Chilli Dog Rolls

This is a variation on the Cheesy Sausage Rolls recipe and perfect for those who like a bit of a kick to their savoury dishes. Make them as hot or as mild as your taste dictates.

• Sift the flour into a bowl and add the salt, paprika and cayenne pepper. Season with black pepper.
• Stir in the chopped chillies and, if using, the grated cheese.
• In a jug, add the milk, oil, Tabasco and egg and beat until combined. Pour this onto the flour and mix to form a dough. The dough needs to be soft but not so sticky that it sticks to the surface. Add more flour if necessary.
• Place on a floured surface and roll to a thickness of about 4–5mm. Cut into rectangles large enough to roll the sausages in.
• Roll up the sausages in the dough and place seam-side down on a greased browning tray. Glaze with egg or milk and a sprinkle of sesame seeds.
• Preheat the halogen oven using the preheat setting or set the temperature to 210°C.
• Place on the high rack and cook for 15 minutes until golden. Check the undersides of the rolls to see if they are browned enough (I use the browning tray as it helps to brown them). If they are not done to your satisfaction, carefully turn them over and cook for another couple of minutes.
• Serve hot or cold.

Puffed Sausage Rolls

SERVES 12-18

- Roll the sausage meat into a thumb-thick length.
- Roll out the pastry to the desired size and thickness (it should be just over twice as wide as your roll of sausage meat, and 1cm longer at each end).
- Place the sausage mix 1–2cm from the long edge of the pastry.
- Coat the edges of the pastry with beaten egg before folding it over the sausage meat. Press down firmly on the edge before cutting the sausage rolls to the desired length.
- Preheat the halogen oven using the preheat setting or turn on to 210°C.
- Place the sausage rolls on a baking tray. Brush with beaten egg and sprinkle with sesame seeds before placing on the high rack and baking for 20–25 minutes, until golden brown. If the undersides of the sausage rolls are not done to your satisfaction or the tops start to darken too quickly, carefully turn them over for the last 5–10 minutes of the cooking time.

1 pack readymade puff or shortcrust pastry
350–400g sausage meat
Beaten egg to glaze
Sprinkle of sesame seeds (optional)

Variations
For a great variation to the standard sausage roll, add some mixed herbs to the sausage meat to create delicious Herby Sausage Rolls. If you like things hot, mix your sausage meat with some fresh chillies and a dash of Tabasco sauce to create tempting Hot, Hot, Hot Sausage Rolls. Vegetarians can opt for any of the above by using vegetarian sausage mix.

Love Hate Cheesy Spins

175g plain flour
½ teaspoon mustard
  powder
1 teaspoon paprika
Seasoning to taste
50g butter
75g mature cheese,
  grated
1 egg, beaten
Marmite
Milk
Sesame seeds

If you love Marmite you will adore these cheesy spins. Light cheesy dough rolled up with extra cheese and Marmite – very yummy and perfect for a picnic or packed lunch.

• Sift the flour into a bowl and add the mustard powder, paprika and seasoning and combine well.
• Rub in the butter before adding two thirds of the grated cheese, in a similar way to making scones.
• Add the beaten egg and combine until you have made a pliable dough. Leave to rest for 5 minutes in the fridge before continuing.
• Roll out the dough onto a floured surface to a 5mm thickness. Once it's at the desired size, spread with Marmite and sprinkle with the remaining cheese.
• Carefully roll up to form a sausage. Then use a sharp serrated knife to cut slices of about 5–8mm thick.
• Preheat the halogen oven using the preheat setting or set the temperature to 180°C.
• Place flat on a browning tray. Brush with milk and sprinkle with sesame seeds.
• Bake on the high rack for 15–20 minutes until golden.
• Place on a cooling rack to cool before serving.

Cheese Biscuits

Nice and light cheese biscuits – perfect for a quick savoury snack. Make them as thin or thick as your taste dictates.

- Place the flour, cayenne pepper and seasoning in a bowl and combine.
- Rub in the butter and grated cheese. Add a little cold water until you have formed a firm, but not too wet, dough. Place in the fridge for half an hour to chill.
- Roll out onto a floured surface to your desired thickness – I prefer them to be very thin as they make lighter biscuits.
- Preheat the halogen oven using the preheat setting or set the temperature to 190°C.
- Cut the dough into shapes with biscuit cutters. Place onto a greased baking tray.
- Place on the low rack and cook for 8–12 minutes, depending on thickness. They should be golden brown.
- Leave on the tray to cool for a minute or two before transferring to a cooling rack.

120g flour
Pinch of cayenne
 pepper
Sprinkle of sea salt
Sprinkle of black
 pepper
40g butter
50g mature Cheddar,
 grated
25g red Leicester,
 grated

SUITABLE FOR VEGETARIANS

Red Onion and Goat's Cheese Upside Down Tart

4 red onions, sliced
Sprinkle of sugar
Sprinkle of sea salt
Drizzle of olive oil
(approximately 1
tablespoon)
Drizzle of balsamic
vinegar
1–2 garlic cloves
(optional)
250g self-raising flour
½ teaspoon baking
powder
50g butter
175ml natural yoghurt
1 teaspoon wholegrain
mustard
110g goat's cheese,
crumbled
Black pepper
A little milk or beaten
egg
Sesame seeds
(optional)

SUITABLE FOR VEGETARIANS

I love this combination – sweet, roasted red onions combined with the distinct flavour of goat's cheese, with a light scone topping (or should I say base as we flip it up when serving!). Serve with a lovely rocket salad for a delicious light lunch or supper.

• Preheat the halogen oven using the preheat setting or set the temperature to 180°C.
• Place the sliced onions in the bottom of a pie dish. Sprinkle with sugar and salt, drizzle with oil and a dash of balsamic vinegar. If you like garlic, crush a clove or two into this mixture. Stir well, ensuring everything is evenly coated in the oil and balsamic.
• Place on the low rack and cook for 20 minutes until the onions are soft.
• Whilst that is cooking you can prepare the scone mix. Sift the flour and baking powder into a bowl. Rub in the butter until it resembles breadcrumbs.
• Add the yoghurt and wholegrain mustard and mix.
• Place on a floured surface and roll or press until you have the same size and shape as your pie dish. Once you are happy with this, and the onions are ready, crumble goat's cheese on top of the onions and season with black pepper before placing the dough over the pie. Press down gently around the edges to seal. Brush with a little milk or beaten egg and sprinkle with sesame seeds if you prefer.
• Place on the low rack and cook for 20–25 minutes or until the dough is golden and firm.

- Remove from the oven. Place a serving plate, slightly larger than your pie dish, over the top of the baked pie, face down, and turn over, so the serving plate is now on the bottom and you are able to remove the pie dish. You will now see the baked onions and goat's cheese on the top with the dough mixture on the bottom.
- Garnish with some crumbled goat's cheese and fresh herbs if preferred.
- Serve immediately – yummy!

The Bakery
– Bread and More . . .

'Pat-a-cake, pat-a-cake, baker's man, bake me a cake as fast as you can, pat it and prick it, and mark it with B, put it in the oven for baby and me.'
– Tom D'Urfey, *The Campaigners* (1698)

Although I have a bread maker, I could not resist trying to make bread in the halogen oven. The whole process of making bread by hand is so good for the soul. You can pound and knead away your troubles whilst listening to your favourite radio show. The joy of making bread in the halogen is viewing the process through the glass bowl – kids also love seeing the magic dough rise and turn golden before their very eyes. If like me, you have a bread maker and don't want to go through the whole kneading process by hand, you can let the bread machine do that for you, then sculpt and shape the dough to your desired shape and cook it in the halogen – ideal also for lovely bread rolls and other doughy delights.

Proving
Some people opt for a single prove – I prefer double as this was the traditional way I was taught, but it is entirely up to you. Personally I find that if I'm using dried yeast it is often better to double prove. Fresh yeast works well

for a single prove. If you want to leave out the second prove, that is fine and will not detract from the overall perfection of your bread. Instead of leaving to prove in the bowl, place the dough in your tin or chosen shape and prove just once before placing in the oven.

You can also prove in your halogen oven. If you are using a digital oven, set the temperature to the wash setting but turn the fan down to low. If you are using a dial setting like the JML, set halfway between the wash and thaw setting.

Extension ring
It may be necessary to use an extension ring when cooking loaves to allow for extra room and to prevent the top of the loaf from browning too quickly.

White Bread

475g white flour
Pinch of salt
30g butter
2 teaspoons sugar
7g dried yeast
300ml warm milk

SUITABLE FOR VEGETARIANS

- Place the flour in a bowl. Add the salt and rub in the butter. Add the sugar and dried yeast and combine well.
- I normally proceed next on a worktop, but you can work in a bowl if you find it easier. I place the flour on the worktop and make a large well in the centre. Pour the warm milk into the centre, then gradually stir in the edges of the flour until it is all mixed in to form a dough. If the dough is too dry, add a little more milk – if too wet, a little more flour. Bread making is all about touch and feel, so enjoy the freedom.
- On the floured surface, knead the dough. For those who have never kneaded before, you fold over the outer edge of the dough back into the middle and

press down with your knuckles. Twist the dough around and repeat this process, continuing to press down and twist as you go, locking in air and stretching the dough for about 10 minutes (a great workout!).

- Place the dough back in the bowl and cover with cling film. Set in a warm, draught-free area and leave until it has doubled in size.
- Return the dough to the floured surface and knead again. You will notice that the dough is lighter and might fall back when you start to knead – don't worry, it will rise again.
- Knead for another 5 minutes and, when you're happy with it, place in a greased loaf tin, or if you are making a round, freeform shape, place this on a baking tray.
- Leave again in a warm place for another 15 minutes until it starts to rise.
- When it is almost ready, preheat the halogen oven using the preheat setting or set the temperature to 200°C.
- Brush the dough with a little warm milk. If you would like the split loaf effect, you can use a sharp knife to score lengthways down the top of the loaf. When cooking, this will split open.
- Place on the low rack and cook for approximately 20–25 minutes until the bread has risen, is firm, and if you tap the bottom of the bread it makes a sound like a drum. If the top of the bread starts to become too dark you can add an extension ring, which will effectively lift the element away from the top of the loaf. If you are making bread rolls using this recipe, they will take 12–15 minutes.
- Place on a cooling rack and resist the temptation to eat before it has cooled.

300ml warm milk or
water
1 dessertspoon malt
extract
1 teaspoon poppy
seeds
2–3 tablespoons
sesame seeds
2–3 tablespoons
sunflower seeds
3 tablespoons golden
linseeds
475g granary or
malted flour
Pinch of salt
30g butter
2 teaspoons sugar
7g dried yeast

SUITABLE FOR VEGETARIANS

Multi-seed Bread

This is one of our favourites. It is actually quite hard to stick to a recipe as we normally chuck any seeds, flax and malt in willy nilly, but here is the basic format which I hope you will enjoy.

- In a jug, mix the warm milk and the malt extract together.
- Place the seeds and flour in a bowl. Add the salt and rub in the butter. Add the sugar and dried yeast and combine well.
- I normally proceed next on a worktop, but you can work in a bowl if you find it easier. I place the flour on the worktop and make a large well in the centre. Pour the warm milk mixture into the centre then gradually stir in the edges of the flour until it is all mixed in to form a dough. If the dough is too dry, add a little more liquid – if too wet, a little more flour. Bread making is all about touch and feel, so enjoy the freedom.
- On the floured surface, knead the dough. For those who have never kneaded before, you fold over the outer edge of the dough back into the middle and press down with your knuckles. Twist the dough around and repeat this process, continuing to press down and twist as you go, locking in air and stretching the dough for about 10 minutes (a great workout!).
- Place the dough back in the bowl and cover with cling film. Set in a warm, draught-free area and leave until it has doubled in size.

- Return the dough to the floured surface and knead again. You will notice that the dough is lighter and might fall back when you start to knead – don't worry, it will rise again.
- Knead for another 5 minutes and, when you're happy with it, place in a greased loaf tin, or if you are making a round, freeform shape, place this on a baking tray.
- Leave again in a warm place for another 15 minutes until it starts to rise.
- When it is almost ready, preheat the halogen oven using the preheat setting or set the temperature to 200°C.
- Brush the dough with a little warm milk.
- Place on the low rack and cook for approximately 20 minutes until the bread has risen, is firm, and if you tap the bottom of the bread it makes a sound like a drum. If you are making bread rolls using this recipe, they will take 12–15 minutes.
- Place on a cooling rack and resist the temptation to eat before it has cooled.

Breakfast Fruit Bread

300ml warm milk

1 tablespoon malt extract

3 tablespoons golden linseeds

120g good quality, nut-free muesli

2 teaspoons mixed spice

25g chopped dates

Pinch of salt

30g butter

3 teaspoons sugar

7g dried yeast

SUITABLE FOR VEGETARIANS

- In a jug, mix the warm milk and malt extract together.
- Place the seeds, muesli, spice, dates and flour in a bowl. Add the salt and rub in the butter. Add the sugar and dried yeast and combine well.
- I normally proceed next on a worktop, but you can work in a bowl if you find it easier. I place the flour mix on the worktop and make a large well in the centre. Pour the warm milk mixture into the centre then gradually stir in the edges of the flour until it is all mixed in to form a dough. If the dough is too dry, add a little more liquid – if too wet, a little more flour. Bread making is all about touch and feel, so enjoy the freedom.
- On the floured surface, knead the dough. For those who have never kneaded before, you fold over the outer edge of the dough back into the middle and press down with your knuckles. Twist the dough around and repeat this process, continuing to press down and twist as you go, locking in air and stretching the dough for about 10 minutes (a great workout!).
- Place the dough back in the bowl and cover with cling film. Set in a warm, draught-free area and leave until it has doubled in size.
- Return the dough to the floured surface and knead again. You will notice that the dough is lighter and might fall back when you start to knead – don't worry, it will rise again.

- Knead for another 5 minutes and, when you're happy with it, place in your greased loaf tin, or if you are making a round, freeform shape, place this on a baking tray.
- Leave again in a warm place for another 15 minutes until it starts to rise.
- When it is almost ready, preheat the halogen oven using the preheat setting or set the temperature to 200°C.
- Brush the dough with a little warm milk or if you want a sticky glaze, dissolve 30g of sugar in a little hot water and brush on.
- Place on the low rack and cook for approximately 20 minutes until the bread has risen, is firm, and if you tap the bottom of the bread it makes a sound like a drum. If you are making bread rolls using this recipe, they will take 12–15 minutes.
- Place on a cooling rack and resist the temptation to eat before it has cooled.

Onion and Herb Bread

200ml warm milk
50ml olive oil
1 large onion, finely
   chopped
Small handful of herbs
   such as chives,
   oregano or thyme,
   freshly chopped
475g white flour
1 teaspoon salt
30g butter
3 teaspoons sugar
7g dried yeast

SUITABLE FOR VEGETARIANS

- In a jug, mix the warm milk and olive oil together.
- Place the onion, herbs and flour in a bowl. Add the salt and rub in the butter. Add the sugar and dried yeast and combine well.
- I normally proceed next on a worktop, but you can work in a bowl if you find it easier. I place the flour on the worktop and make a large well in the centre. Pour the warm milk mixture into the centre then gradually stir in the edges of the flour until it is all mixed in to form a dough. If the dough is too dry, add a little more liquid – if too wet, a little more flour. Bread making is all about touch and feel, so enjoy the freedom.
- On the floured surface, knead the dough. For those who have never kneaded before, you fold over the outer edge of the dough back into the middle and press down with your knuckles. Twist the dough around and repeat this process, continuing to press down and twist as you go, locking in air and stretching the dough for about 10 minutes (a great workout!).
- Place the dough back in the bowl and cover with cling film. Set in a warm, draught-free area and leave until it has doubled in size.
- Return the dough to the floured surface and knead again. You will notice that the dough is lighter and might fall back when you start to knead – don't worry, it will rise again.

- Knead for another 5 minutes, and when you're happy with it, place in your greased loaf tin, or if you are making a round, freeform shape, place this on a baking tray.
- Leave again in a warm place for another 15 minutes until it starts to rise.
- When it is almost ready, preheat the halogen oven using the preheat setting or set the temperature to 200°C.
- Brush the dough with a little warm milk.
- Place on the low rack and cook for approximately 20 minutes until the bread has risen, is firm, and if you tap the bottom of the bread it makes a sound like a drum. If you are making bread rolls using this recipe, they will take 12–15 minutes.
- Place on a cooling rack and resist the temptation to eat before it has cooled.

Cheese, Onion and Chive Bread

200ml warm milk

25ml olive oil

1 large onion, finely chopped

50–75g mature cheese, grated

Small handful of chives, freshly chopped

475g white flour

1 teaspoon salt

30g butter

3 teaspoons sugar

7g dried yeast

SUITABLE FOR VEGETARIANS

- In a jug, mix the warm milk and olive oil together.
- Place the onion, cheese, chives and flour in a bowl. Add the salt and rub in the butter. Add the sugar and dried yeast and combine well.
- I normally proceed next on a worktop, but you can work in a bowl if you find it easier. I place the flour on the worktop and make a large well in the centre. Pour the warm milk mixture into the centre then gradually stir in the edges of the flour until it is all mixed in to form a dough. If the dough is too dry, add a little more liquid – if too wet, a little more flour. Bread making is all about touch and feel, so enjoy the freedom.
- On the floured surface, knead the dough. For those who have never kneaded before, you fold over the outer edge of the dough back into the middle and press down with your knuckles. Twist the dough around and repeat this process, continuing to press down and twist as you go, locking in air and stretching the dough for about 10 minutes (a great workout!).
- Place the dough back in the bowl and cover with cling film. Set in a warm, draught-free area and leave until it has doubled in size.
- Return the dough to the floured surface and knead again. You will notice that the dough is lighter and might fall back when you start to knead – don't worry, it will rise again.
- Knead for another 5 minutes, and when you're happy with it, place in your greased loaf tin, or if you are making a round, freeform shape, place this on a baking tray.

- Leave again in a warm place for another 15 minutes until it starts to rise.
- When it is almost ready, preheat the halogen oven using the preheat setting or set the temperature to 200°C.
- Brush the dough with a little warm milk.
- Place on the low rack and cook for approximately 20 minutes until the bread has risen, is firm, and if you tap the bottom of the bread it makes a sound like a drum. If you are making bread rolls using this recipe, they will take 12–15 minutes.
- Place on a cooling rack and resist the temptation to eat before it has cooled.

Sundried Tomato, Garlic and Herb Flat Bread

225g white flour

2–3 cloves of garlic, crushed

1 small red onion, finely sliced

50g sundried tomatoes, chopped

Small handful of thyme, rosemary or oregano, freshly chopped

Pinch of salt

20g butter

2 teaspoons sugar

½ of a 7g packet of dried yeast

1–2 teaspoons sundried tomato paste

150ml warm milk

Drizzle of olive oil

SUITABLE FOR VEGETARIANS

- Place the flour in a bowl. Add the garlic and the onion, tomatoes and herbs, reserving a little of each for the top of the bread. Add the salt and rub in the butter. Add the sugar and dried yeast and combine well.
- I normally proceed next on a worktop, but you can work in a bowl if you find it easier. I place the flour on the worktop and make a large well in the centre.
- Add the sundried tomato paste to the warm milk and mix to combine. Pour the warm milk into the centre and then gradually stir in the edges of the flour until it is all mixed in to form a dough. If the dough is too dry, add a little more liquid – if too wet, a little more flour. Bread making is all about touch and feel, so enjoy the freedom.
- On the floured surface, knead the dough. For those who have never kneaded before, you fold over the outer edge of the dough back into the middle and press down with your knuckles. Twist the dough around and repeat this process, continuing to press down and twist as you go, locking in air and stretching the dough for about 10 minutes (a great workout!).
- Place the dough back in the bowl and cover with cling film. Set in a warm, draught-free area and leave until it has doubled in size.
- Return the dough to the floured surface and knead again. You will notice that the dough is lighter and might fall back when you start to knead – don't worry, it will rise again.

- Preheat the halogen oven using the preheat setting or set the temperature to 200°C.
- Knead for another 5 minutes and, when you're happy with it, roll into a flat square or circle. Place this on a baking tray. Press the remaining fresh herbs, onion and tomatoes into the dough before drizzling with a little olive oil.
- Place the bread on the low rack and cook for approximately 20 minutes until it has risen.
- Place on a cooling rack and resist the temptation to eat before it has cooled.

Sundried Tomato and Oregano Bread

475g white or
   wholemeal flour
Pinch of salt
30g butter
2 teaspoons sugar
7g dried yeast
300ml warm milk
2 tablespoons
   sundried tomato
   purée
1 tablespoon olive oil
2 teaspoons dried
   oregano
100g sundried
   tomatoes in oil
   (drained)
Seeds to sprinkle
   (poppy, sunflower or
   pumpkin seeds)

SUITABLE FOR VEGETARIANS

- Place the flour in a bowl. Add the salt and rub in the butter. Add the sugar and dried yeast and combine well.
- Add the sundried tomato purée, olive oil, oregano and sundried tomatoes (reserving some for the top of the bread if desired) to the milk and combine.
- I normally proceed next on a worktop, but you can work in a bowl or food mixer if you find it easier. I place the flour on the worktop and make a large well in the centre. Pour the warm milk mixture into the centre then gradually stir in the edges of the flour until it is all mixed in to form a dough. If the dough is too dry, add a little more liquid – if too wet, a little more flour. Bread making is all about touch and feel, so enjoy the freedom.
- On the floured surface, knead the dough. For those who have never kneaded before, you fold over the outer edge of the dough back into the middle and press down with your knuckles. Twist the dough around and repeat this process, continuing to press down and twist as you go, locking in air and stretching the dough for about 10 minutes (a great workout!).
- Place the dough back in the bowl and cover with cling film. Set in a warm, draught-free area and leave until it has doubled in size.
- Return the dough to the floured surface and knead again. You will notice that the dough is lighter and might fall back when you start to knead – don't worry, it will rise again.

- Knead for another 5 minutes, and when you're happy with it, place in your greased loaf tin, or if you are making a round, freeform shape, place this on a baking tray.
- Leave again in a warm place for another 15 minutes until it starts to rise.
- When almost ready, preheat the halogen oven using the preheat setting or set the temperature to 200°C.
- Brush the bread with a little warm milk and sprinkle with chopped sundried tomatoes or some seeds.
- Place the bread on the low rack and cook for approximately 20–25 minutes until it has risen, is firm, and if you tap the bottom of the bread it makes a sound like a drum. If the top of the bread starts to become too dark you can add an extension ring, which will effectively lift the element away from the top of the loaf. If you are making bread rolls using this recipe, they will take 12–15 minutes.
- Place on a cooling rack and resist the temptation to eat before it has cooled.

Olive and Rosemary Bread

200ml warm milk
25ml olive oil
150g chopped olives
Small handful of
  rosemary, freshly
  chopped
475g white flour
1 teaspoon salt
Black pepper
30g butter
3 teaspoons sugar
7g dried yeast

SUITABLE FOR VEGETARIANS

- In a jug, mix the warm milk and olive oil together.
- Place the olives (reserving some for the top of the bread if desired), rosemary and flour in a bowl. Add the salt and season with black pepper. Rub in the butter. Add the sugar and dried yeast and combine well.
- I normally proceed next on a worktop, but you can work in a bowl if you find it easier. I place the flour on the worktop and make a large well in the centre. Pour the warm milk mixture into the centre, then gradually stir in the edges of the flour until it is all mixed in to form a dough. If the dough is too dry, add a little more liquid – if too wet, a little more flour. Bread making is all about touch and feel, so enjoy the freedom.
- On the floured surface, knead the dough. For those who have never kneaded before, you fold over the outer edge of the dough back into the middle and press down with your knuckles. Twist the dough around and repeat this process, continuing to press down and twist as you go, locking in air and stretching the dough for about 10 minutes (a great workout!).
- Place the dough back in the bowl and cover with cling film. Set in a warm, draught-free area and leave until it has doubled in size.
- Return the dough to the floured surface and knead again. You will notice that the dough is lighter and might fall back when you start to knead – don't worry, it will rise again.

- Knead for another 5 minutes and, when you're happy with it, place in your greased loaf tin, or if you are making a round, freeform shape, place this on a baking tray.
- Leave again in a warm place for another 15 minutes until it starts to rise.
- When almost ready, preheat the halogen oven using the preheat setting or set the temperature to 200°C.
- Brush the dough with a little warm milk or sprinkle with chopped olives.
- Place on the low rack and cook for approximately 20 minutes until the bread has risen, is firm, and if you tap the bottom of the bread it makes a sound like a drum. If you are making bread rolls using this recipe, they will take 12–15 minutes.
- Place on a cooling rack and resist the temptation to eat before it has cooled.

SERVES 4-6

Basic Dough
500g strong bread
  flour
325ml warm water
7g dried yeast
1 teaspoon brown
  sugar
2 tablespoons olive oil

SUITABLE FOR VEGETARIANS OR
VEGANS (DEPENDING ON
CHOSEN TOPPINGS)

Homemade Pizza

To save time, you could make your own dough in advance. Roll it out and place each piece on greased foil or a parchment sheet. Stack the pizza bases on top of each other, cover in cling film or foil and refrigerate until ready to use.

• Sift the flour into a bowl.
• Mix the water, yeast, sugar and oil together. Make sure the sugar is dissolved. Make a well in the middle of the flour and pour in.
• Mix thoroughly before transferring the dough onto a floured board. Knead well until the dough springs back when pulled.
• Place the dough in a floured bowl and cover with cling film or a warm, damp cloth until it has doubled in size. This takes about 1 hour.
• Knead again, and divide into individual pizza bases or as preferred. This dough can be stored in the fridge or freezer until needed.

Basic Pizza Topping

Pizza topping can be made using pasta sauce or even simple tomato purée mixed with olive oil and herbs. There are no hard and fast rules for pizza toppings so experiment with whatever you fancy and have fun. Below are some suggestions to help you but, really, anything goes!

- Tomato and cheese
- Pepperoni, mushrooms, red onions and cheese
- Ham and mushroom
- Ham, pineapple and cheese
- Chorizo, jalapenos, tomato and cheese
- Red onions, black olives, tomatoes, cheese and red peppers
- Roasted vegetables

Bake Your Pizza
- Once your dough has proved, roll out to the desired thickness and size. Cover with your preferred toppings, starting with the tomato base.
- I normally cook my pizza on the browning tray as I like the bottom to crisp, but you can place it on a tray, on foil or directly on the rack.
- Turn your halogen oven to 200°C and cook for 10–15 minutes on the high rack until golden.
- Due to the force of the fan, if you have loose toppings you may want to place the low rack face down on top of the pizza. I suggest you spray with a little oil to prevent sticking. You only need to do this for the first half of the cooking time.

SERVES 4-6

1 punnet cherry
  tomatoes, halved
2–3 cloves of garlic,
  crushed
1 red onion, sliced
Handful of basil
  leaves, crushed
1 teaspoon salt
1 teaspoon sugar
Drizzle of olive oil
1 ball of mozzarella or
  80g goat's cheese,
  crumbled (omit if
  vegan and substitute
  with vegan cheese if
  desired)

Basic Dough
500g strong bread
  flour
325ml warm water
7g dried yeast
1 teaspoon brown
  sugar
2 tablespoons olive oil

SUITABLE FOR VEGETARIANS
OR VEGANS

Upside Down Pizza Bake

This is a really nice dish and makes a change from the normal pizza. It uses the same principle as an upside down cake. I love the flavour of the slow cooked tomatoes – ideal for using up some soft tomatoes. This recipe uses cherry tomatoes, but feel free to use a variety of your choice.

- Prepare the dough by sifting the flour into a bowl.
- Mix the water, yeast, sugar and oil together. Make sure the sugar is dissolved. Make a well in the middle of the flour and pour in.
- Mix thoroughly before transferring the dough onto a floured board. Knead well until the dough springs back when pulled.
- Place the dough in a floured bowl and cover with cling film or a warm, damp cloth until it has doubled in size. This takes about 1 hour.
- Place the tomatoes, garlic, onion, basil, salt, sugar and olive oil in a deep-sided baking tray (ideally a round tray so you can turn it out on a serving plate when complete, but make sure it fits in your halogen cooker!).
- Cook at 130–140°C for 30–60 minutes.
- Knead again. Roll out to form the same size as your baking tray (you will later place the dough inside the tray to form a top). You may have more dough than needed – it depends on how thick you want the crust of the bake. If you have some left over, you can roll it out to make a pizza base, cover in greased foil or parchment and freeze for another day.

- Remove the baked tomatoes from the halogen oven and turn it up to 210°C. You can top the tomatoes with the dough, or cheese lovers may like to add some crumbled mozzarella or even goat's cheese onto the tomatoes before adding the dough.
- Place this back into the halogen oven and bake on high rack for 15–20 minutes until the top is golden.
- To serve, place a plate, slightly larger than the top of the baking tray, over the dough, face down, ready to flip up, displaying the tomato base on top of the pizza dough.
- Serve with green salad.

Savoury Spin Wheels

MAKES 10–14

225g bread flour
2 teaspoons sugar
7g dried yeast
30g butter
1 large egg, beaten
125ml warm milk
1 tablespoon sundried
   tomato paste
50–75g mature cheese,
   grated
1 onion, finely
   chopped
1–2 teaspoons oregano
50g bacon or pancetta
   (optional)

- In a large bowl, add the flour, sugar and dried yeast. Combine well.
- Rub in the butter to form a texture similar to breadcrumbs. Once combined, add the egg and warm milk. Combine well to form a dough.
- On a floured surface, knead the dough for 5 minutes. Then place the dough back in the bowl, cover and keep in a warm place for 30–40 minutes or until it has doubled in size.
- Preheat the halogen oven using the preheat setting or set the temperature to 180°C.
- When the dough is ready, place it back on the floured surface and knead again for another 5 minutes.
- Roll into a large rectangle of roughly 30cm, making sure there are no breaks in the dough.
- Leaving a gap of approximately 2cm around the edge, cover the dough with a thin layer of sundried tomato paste.
- Sprinkle with the grated cheese, finely chopped onion, oregano and bacon.
- Holding the end of the dough nearest to you, gently lift and roll to create a large sausage.
- Using a sharp serrated knife, cut 2cm slices. Place these on a well-greased or lined baking tray.
- Place in the halogen oven on the low rack. (You may need to do this in batches or use an extension ring to enable you to use two racks, though cooking times will vary as the top rack will cook quicker than the bottom rack.)
- Cook for 20–25 minutes until golden and risen.
- Serve hot or cold.

Chocolate and Hazelnut Wheels

MAKES 10–14

- In a large bowl, add the flour, sugar and dried yeast. Combine well.
- Rub in the butter to form a texture similar to breadcrumbs. Once combined, add the egg and warm milk. Combine well to form a dough.
- On a floured surface, knead the dough for 5 minutes. Then place the dough back in the bowl, cover and keep in a warm place for 30–40 minutes or until it has doubled in size.
- Preheat the halogen oven using the preheat setting or set the temperature to 180°C.
- When the dough is ready, place it back on the floured surface and knead again for another 5 minutes.
- Roll into a large rectangle, roughly 30cm, making sure there are no breaks in the dough.
- Leaving a gap of approximately 2cm around the edge, cover the dough with chocolate spread. Finish with the chopped hazelnuts and chocolate chips, ensuring they are evenly distributed.
- Holding the end of the dough nearest to you, gently lift and roll to create a large sausage.
- Using a sharp serrated knife, cut 2cm slices. Place these on a well-greased or lined baking tray.
- Place in the halogen oven on the low rack. (You may need to do this in batches or use an extension ring to enable you to use two racks, though cooking times will vary as the top rack will cook quicker than the bottom rack.)
- Cook for 20–25 minutes until golden and risen.
- Serve hot or cold.

225g bread flour
40g sugar
7g dried yeast
30g butter
1 large egg, beaten
125ml warm milk
2 tablespoons chocolate spread (such as Nutella)
50g chopped hazelnuts
50g dark chocolate chips

SUITABLE FOR VEGETARIANS

MAKES 10–14

225g bread flour
2 teaspoons sugar
7g dried yeast
30g butter
1 large egg, beaten
125ml warm milk
30g butter
50–75g dried fruit
40g brown sugar
2 teaspoons cinnamon
Sprinkle of sugar to
   decorate

SUITABLE FOR VEGETARIANS

Chelsea Buns

- In a large bowl, add the flour, sugar and dried yeast. Combine well.
- Rub in the butter to form a texture similar to breadcrumbs. Once combined, add the egg and warm milk. Combine well to form a dough.
- On a floured surface, knead the dough for 5 minutes. Then place the dough back in the bowl, cover and keep in a warm place for 30–40 minutes or until it has doubled in size.
- Preheat the halogen oven using the preheat setting or set the temperature to 180°C.
- When the dough is ready, place it back on the floured surface and knead again for another 5 minutes.
- Roll into a large rectangle, roughly 30cm, making sure there are no breaks in the dough.
- Melt the remaining 30g of butter, either with the heat of the halogen oven or in a saucepan (though make sure it does not burn).
- Leaving a gap of approximately 2cm around the edge, brush the dough with melted butter. Finish by evenly distributing the dried fruit, brown sugar and cinnamon.
- Holding the end of the dough nearest to you, gently lift and roll to create a large sausage.
- Using a sharp serrated knife, cut 2cm slices. Place these on a well-greased or lined baking tray. It is fine to place them so that they touch when risen, as you can pull them apart when cooked.

- Place in the halogen oven on the low rack. (You may need to do this in batches or use an extension ring to enable you to use two racks, though cooking times will vary as the top rack will cook quicker than the bottom rack.)
- Cook for 20–25 minutes until golden and risen. Remove and place on a cooling rack.
- Sprinkle with sugar before serving hot or cold.

Tasty Malt Loaf

1 teaspoon dried yeast
175ml warm milk
375g bread flour
2 tablespoons dark
brown or muscovado
sugar
2 teaspoons cinnamon
Zest of 1 orange
90g raisins
90g sultanas
15g chopped dates
3–4 tablespoons malt
extract
1 tablespoon olive oil
1–2 tablespoons sugar
to glaze (optional)

SUITABLE FOR VEGETARIANS

- Place the yeast and milk in a jug and add 1 teaspoon of the sugar to help activate. Leave to one side until it starts to become frothy.
- Meanwhile, put the flour, sugar, cinnamon, orange zest and dried fruit in a bowl and combine well.
- Mix the malt and the olive oil with the frothy milk and yeast mix. Pour this mixture into the mixing bowl and combine well with the dried ingredients. Combine well to form a dough.
- On a floured surface, knead the dough for 5 minutes. Place the dough back in the bowl, cover and keep in a warm place for 30–40 minutes or until it has doubled in size.
- Knead again before placing in a greased 1lb (0.5kg) loaf tin. Leave to rise again for another 20 minutes.
- When the dough is ready, preheat the halogen oven to 200°C.
- Place the loaf on the low rack and cook for 25–30 minutes. If it starts to get too dark on top, add an extension ring to lift the element away from the top of the bread.
- Once cooked and whilst it is still warm, you can make a sticky glaze by heating equal parts sugar to water. I normally use 1–2 tablespoons of each. Heat gently but bring up to the boil, stirring well. Once it has simmered for a minute or two, you can carefully use it to glaze the loaf. Be aware that the glaze is very hot and will cause a nasty burn if you get any on your skin, so brush with care.
- Leave to cool before slicing. Delicious!

Apple, Chocolate and Hazelnut Pizza

- In a large bowl, add the flour, sugar and dried yeast. Combine well.
- Rub in the butter to form a texture similar to breadcrumbs. Once combined, add the egg and warm milk. Combine well to form a dough.
- On a floured surface, knead the dough for 5 minutes. Then place it back in the bowl, cover and keep in a warm place for 30–40 minutes or until it has doubled in size.
- Preheat the halogen oven using the preheat setting or set the temperature to 180°C.
- When the dough is ready, place it back on the floured surface and knead again for another 5 minutes.
- Roll to size and press into a greased tin. It should fit into one or two pizza dishes, depending on the size of your dish.
- Spread or add a few small dollops of the chocolate spread to the centre of the pizza dough, leaving about a 10mm gap around the edges.
- Slice the peeled apples. Sprinkle with a little lemon juice to stop them going brown.
- Place the apple slices over the chocolate spread, sprinkle with sugar and finish with the chopped hazelnuts and chocolate chips.
- Place on the low rack and cook for 15–20 minutes until golden.
- Serve immediately with whipped cream or crème fraîche.

225g bread flour
2 teaspoons sugar
7g dried yeast
30g butter
1 large egg, beaten
125ml warm milk
Chocolate spread
3–4 cooking apples, peeled
Lemon juice
2 tablespoons sugar
30g hazelnuts, chopped
40g dark chocolate chips

SUITABLE FOR VEGETARIANS

Date and Walnut Bread

200ml warm milk
1 tablespoon malt
  extract
350g white flour
75g walnuts, roughly
  chopped
75g dates, chopped
Zest of 1 orange
Pinch of salt
30g butter
3 teaspoons sugar
7g dried yeast
Extra warm milk or
  30g sugar to glaze

SUITABLE FOR VEGETARIANS

- In a jug, mix the warm milk and malt extract together.
- Place the flour, walnuts, dates and zest in a bowl. Add the salt and rub in the butter. Add the sugar and dried yeast and combine well.
- I normally proceed next on a worktop, but you can work in a bowl if you find it easier. I place the flour on the worktop and make a large well in the centre. Pour the warm milk mixture into the centre then gradually stir in the edges of the flour until it is all mixed in to form a dough. If the dough is too dry, add a little more liquid – if too wet, a little more flour. Bread making is all about touch and feel, so enjoy the freedom.
- On the floured surface, knead the dough. For those who have never kneaded before, you fold over the outer edge of the dough back into the middle and press down with your knuckles. Twist the dough around and repeat this process, continuing to press down and twist as you go, locking in air and stretching the dough for about 10 minutes (a great workout!).
- Place the dough back in the bowl and cover with cling film. Set in a warm, draught-free area and leave until it has doubled in size.
- Return the dough to the floured surface and knead again. You will notice that the dough is lighter and might fall back when you start to knead – don't worry, it will rise again.

- Knead for another 5 minutes, and when you're happy with it, place in your greased loaf tin, or if you are making a round, freeform shape, place this on a baking tray.
- Leave again in a warm place for another 15 minutes until it starts to rise.
- When the dough is almost ready, preheat the halogen oven using the preheat setting or set the temperature to 200°C.
- Brush the dough with a little warm milk or, if you want a sticky glaze, dissolve 30g of sugar with a little hot water and brush on.
- Place the bread on the low rack and cook for approximately 20–25 minutes until the bread has risen, is firm, and if you tap the bottom of the bread it makes a sound like a drum. If it starts to get too dark on top add the extension ring, which will lift the element away from the top of the bread. If you are making bread rolls using this recipe, they will take 12–15 minutes.
- Place on a cooling rack and resist the temptation to eat before it has cooled.

Toasted Tea Cakes

7g dried yeast

50g sugar

225ml warm milk or
water

350g plain flour

50g butter

50g currants

1–2 teaspoons
cinnamon or mixed
spice

1–2 tablespoons sugar
to glaze

SUITABLE FOR VEGETARIANS

This is a recipe passed on to me from my great aunt. I found it
in her recipe book but it was called Currant Toasted Buns. I
have adapted it by adding some spice, but if you prefer the
original 1940s/50s-style recipe, omit the spice.

• In a jug, put the dried yeast and 1 teaspoon of sugar.
  Add the water or warm milk and leave to activate.
• Meanwhile sift the flour into a bowl. Rub in the
  butter before adding the rest of the sugar, currants
  and spices. Combine well.
• Once the yeast has activated, pour onto the flour and
  combine to form a dough. You can use your mixer for
  this but I prefer to get my hands in the dough –
  much more satisfying!
• Place the dough onto a floured surface and knead for
  10 minutes. Once kneaded, place it back in the bowl,
  cover with cling film and leave to prove. You can use
  your halogen oven to prove by placing the dough on
  a baking tray and setting the timer just between the
  wash and thaw settings (about halfway on a timer or
  on a digital reading, press the wash setting).
• Once it has doubled in size bring the dough back to
  your floured board and knead again for 5 minutes.
  Break the dough into about 12 pieces and form balls.
  Press down to form flatter cakes.
• Place these on a greased baking tray and prove again
  for another 15 minutes.
• Preheat the halogen oven using the preheat setting or
  set the temperature to 200°C.

- Place the buns on the low rack (you will have to cook in batches or use an extension ring to create two shelves).
- Cook for 12–15 minutes until golden.
- Place on a cooling rack to cool. If you prefer a sticky glaze to your buns, mix equal parts water and sugar together (1–2 tablespoons of each should be enough). Heat in a saucepan until dissolved then brush onto the warm buns. Leave to cool.
- Serve with a little butter or toast for a delicious afternoon tea snack.

Cupcakes, Muffins and Fairy Dust

'I look at them as a child looks at a cake, with glittering eyes and watering mouth, imagining the pleasure that awaits him.'
– Elizabeth Gaskell, 1859

There is something wonderfully decadent about eating a tasty cupcake decorated with thick icing and sprinkles. I love the fact that you can make cupcakes or muffins in minutes and, with the help of a food mixer, really with the minimum of effort. You can buy wonderful cupcake stands or ornate and vintage cake stands, perfect for displaying your wonderful creations.

If you have children and want a quick, easy snack or have to create cakes for the school cake stand, these are perfect for you. They very rarely go wrong if you follow the simple formula. Sponge cakes use equal quantities of fat, sugar and self-raising flour. When we measured in ounces, it was easy to remember: 4 ounces of these ingredients needed 2 eggs (i.e. half the ounces), 6 ounces needed 3 eggs and so on. Now we are working in grammes it is not so easy to remember!

Where applicable I have included recipes for icing. I prefer to use cream cheese in my thick icing – it is lovely to pipe onto your cupcakes and gives them a really professional finish. If I colour the icing, I use pastes rather than the nasty cheap colourings available in supermarkets. You can buy these from cook shops or retailers such as Lakeland. Unlike the cheaper varieties, pastes don't overwhelm the icing with liquid. You can add a little at a time to create a wonderful vibrant colour. Alternatively, you could make simple icing by just mixing icing sugar with a few drops of water. Add your paste to create your own colour. For decadent chocolate muffins or cupcakes you could make a chocolate ganache (gently mix equal parts chocolate with cream, heat gently until melted and then use).

The halogen oven is perfect for creating mouth-watering muffins, cupcakes and fairy cakes. I have not managed to find a round muffin tin, but I find silicon muffin cases, placed in a round tin, perfectly adequate. Don't be tempted to use paper cases as these will wilt and lose their shape during the cooking process and you will end up with very flat cakes!

Baking takes 12–20 minutes, depending on the size of your muffins, in a preheated halogen oven. The best way to check if they are cooked is to touch the tops of the cakes with your finger. If they are firm to touch and spring back when you add pressure, they are done. If the middles are a bit soggy, keep them in for a few minutes longer. I have noticed that some halogen cookbooks recommend using foil to prevent burning and turning the temperature up to as much as 230°C. Personally, I can't really understand this approach. Keep the temperature within the normal conventional cooking temperatures and you will have no problems regarding burning tops or soggy middles and your cakes will cook evenly.

If you are using the extension ring and cooking on

two levels, remember that the top cakes will cook faster than the bottom ones so allow for this. I prefer to cook on one level as they only take 10–12 minutes and I can cook 8–10 in one batch.

As with all baking, try to use the best quality ingredients as it really does make a difference. I always sift my flour and beat my eggs before adding. I also use Madagascan vanilla extract or pastes, as these are far better than the cheap imitation vanilla extracts you can buy in supermarkets. Yes, it does cost a lot more but will last you a long time so is well worth the expense.

When adding ingredients, consider how wet they will be. For example, raspberry cupcakes are much wetter than chocolate, so you may need to cook for a little longer to avoid wet middles. When using chocolate chips, remember they will be wet when hot, but will revert to their solid form when cool.

The number of cupcakes each of the following recipes makes will vary according to the size of cupcake cases you use, so I've indicated the range.

Vanilla and Chocolate Chip Fairy Cakes

MAKES 10–18

175g butter
175g sugar
3 eggs, beaten
175g self-raising flour
1 teaspoon vanilla
   essence
50g chocolate chips
   (dark, milk, white or
   combination)

SUITABLE FOR VEGETARIANS

- Preheat the halogen oven using the preheat setting or set to 200°C.
- Cream the butter and sugar together until pale and fluffy.
- Add the eggs and vanilla a little at a time and continue to beat well.
- Sift the flour and fold into the mixture gently.
- When thoroughly mixed, add the chocolate chips and combine.
- Place in cupcake or muffin cases in a muffin/cupcake tray. I have not been able to find a round muffin tray so I use silicon muffin cases and place them on the halogen baking trays that come with the accessory packs. You can comfortably fit 10 on a tray.
- Place on the low rack and cook for 12–18 minutes. The cakes should be firm and spring back when touched.
- Place on a cooling rack to cool. If you are using silicon muffin cases, wait until they are cool, then carefully pull away at the sides of the case. Once clear all the way around, turn upside down and the cake should pop out.

Almond and Raspberry Fairy Cakes

MAKES 8–15

- Cream the butter and sugar together until pale and fluffy.
- Add the eggs a little at a time and continue to beat well. Add the almond essence.
- Sift the flour and almonds and fold into the mixture gently until thoroughly combined.
- Place half the mixture in each cupcake case. Follow this with half a teaspoon of raspberry jam placed in the very centre of the mixture. Then add the final layer of cake mix, ensuring the jam is completely covered.
- Place on the low rack and cook for 12–18 minutes. The cakes should be firm and spring back when touched.
- Place on a cooling rack to cool. If you are using silicon muffin cases, wait until they are cool, then carefully pull away at the sides of the case. Once clear all the way around, turn upside down and the cake should pop out. Leave to cool.
- Once cool, cover the top of the cakes with raspberry jam and finish with a generous sprinkle of coconut.

175g butter
175g sugar
3 eggs, beaten
1 teaspoon almond essence
150g self-raising flour
25g ground almonds
4–7 teaspoons raspberry jam
Extra raspberry jam and desiccated coconut to finish

SUITABLE FOR VEGETARIANS

MAKES 8–12

110g butter
110g brown sugar
2 eggs, beaten
110g self-raising flour
75g raisins or sultanas
   or mixed dried fruit
1 teaspoon spice –
   cinnamon, nutmeg
   or allspice (optional)

SUITABLE FOR VEGETARIANS

Fruit Fairies

It's funny that people don't make the traditional dried fruit fairy cakes any more. When I was growing up they were a favourite and they are so simple to make. Feel free to add some spices or cinnamon to enhance them.

- Preheat the halogen oven using the preheat setting or set to 200°C.
- Cream the butter and sugar together until pale and fluffy.
- Add the eggs a little at a time and continue to beat well.
- Sift the flour and fold into the mixture gently.
- When thoroughly mixed, add the dried fruit and spices (if using) and combine well.
- Place in cupcake or muffin cases on a muffin/cupcake tray. I have not been able to find a round muffin tray so I use silicon muffin cases and place them on the halogen baking trays that come with the accessory packs. You can comfortably fit 10 on a tray.
- Place on the low rack and cook for 15–18 minutes. The cakes should be firm and spring back when touched.
- Place on a cooling rack to cool. If you are using silicon muffin cases, wait until they are cool, then carefully pull away at the sides of the case. Once clear all the way around, turn upside down and the cake should pop out.

Lemon Butterfly Cakes

MAKES 10–18

- Preheat the halogen oven using the preheat setting or set to 200°C.
- Cream the butter and sugar together until pale and fluffy.
- Add the eggs a little at a time and continue to beat well. Then add the lemon zest and lemon juice.
- Sift the flour and fold into the mixture gently. Mix until well combined.
- Place in cupcake or muffin silicon cases and place on a tray. You can comfortably fit 10 on the tray.
- Place on the low rack and cook for 12–18 minutes. The cakes should be firm and spring back when touched.
- Place on a cooling rack to cool. If you are using silicon muffin cases, wait until they are cool, then carefully pull away at the sides of the case. Once clear all the way around, turn upside down and the cake should pop out.
- While the cakes are cooling, prepare the butter icing. Beat the butter until soft. Gradually add the icing sugar. Add a few drops of lemon juice at a time until you reach the desired consistency – it should be glossy, thick and lump free. The best way of testing to see if you have added enough icing sugar is to taste it. It should taste sweet and creamy but not too buttery.
- Take the cakes and using a sharp knife, cut out an arc of cake. Cut in half to create two butterfly wings.
- Fill the hole with a generous dollop of the butter icing. Place the wings on the top of the cakes, on their side, with the top sides facing one another to make the wing shape. Sprinkle with icing sugar.

175g butter
175g sugar
3 eggs, beaten
Zest of 1 lemon
2 teaspoons lemon juice
180g self-raising flour

Butter Icing
50g butter
150–175g icing sugar
Drizzle of lemon juice

SUITABLE FOR VEGETARIANS

Chocolate Butterfly Cakes

MAKES 8–15

50g cocoa
15ml boiling water
175g butter
175g sugar
3 eggs, beaten
175g self-raising flour

Butter Icing
75g butter
150–175g icing sugar
1 teaspoon vanilla
  essence
Drizzle of water

SUITABLE FOR VEGETARIANS

- Preheat the halogen oven using the preheat setting or set to 200°C.
- Mix the cocoa with the hot water and leave to one side.
- Cream the butter and sugar together until pale and fluffy.
- Add the eggs a little at a time and continue to beat well.
- Sift the flour and fold into the mixture gently.
- When thoroughly mixed, add the cocoa mixture and combine.
- Place in silicon cupcake or muffin cases on your baking tray. You can comfortably fit 10 on the tray.
- Place on the low rack and cook for 12–18 minutes. The cakes should be firm and spring back when touched.
- Place on a cooling rack to cool. If you are using silicon muffin cases, wait until they are cool, then carefully pull away at the sides of the case. Once clear all the way around, turn upside down and the cake should pop out.
- While the cakes are cooling, prepare the butter icing. Beat the butter until soft. Gradually add the icing sugar and vanilla essence. Add a few drops of water at a time until you reach the desired consistency – it should be glossy, thick and lump free. The best way of testing to see if you have added enough icing sugar is to taste it. It should taste sweet and creamy but not too buttery.
- Take the cakes and, using a sharp knife, cut out an arc of cake. Cut this in half to create two butterfly wings.

- Fill the hole with butter icing. Place the wings on the top of the cakes, on their side with the top sides facing one another to make the wing shape. Sprinkle with icing sugar and you are ready to serve.

Apple and Date Muffins

- Preheat the halogen oven using the preheat setting or set to 200°C.
- In a bowl combine the flour, cinnamon and sugar.
- Melt the butter and mix with the milk, vanilla and egg. Combine well before mixing with the dry ingredients.
- When thoroughly mixed, add the dates and apple and combine well.
- Place in silicon cupcake or muffin cases. You can comfortably fit 10 on a tray.
- Place on the low rack and cook for 15–18 minutes. The cakes should be firm and spring back when touched.
- Place on a cooling rack to cool or enjoy them warm with a dollop of crème fraîche!

MAKES 10–15

120g self-raising flour
2 teaspoons cinnamon
140g sugar
40g butter
120ml full fat milk or buttermilk
1 teaspoon vanilla extract
1 egg
30g dates, chopped
60g dried apple rings, chopped

SUITABLE FOR VEGETARIANS

MAKES 8–14

125g self-raising flour
50g sugar
75g dried fruit
   (currants, sultanas,
   raisins)
2–3 teaspoons
   cinnamon
½ teaspoon nutmeg
275ml milk
1 egg
4 tablespoons olive oil

SUITABLE FOR VEGETARIANS

Easter Muffins

This is a lovely fruit and spice muffin, which despite its name can be enjoyed at any time of the year!

• Preheat the halogen oven using the preheat setting or set the temperature to 180°C.
• In a mixing bowl, sift the flour and add the other dry ingredients. Combine well.
• Place the milk in a jug and beat in the egg and olive oil. Combine well before pouring into the dry ingredients. Mix thoroughly.
• Place in silicon cupcake or muffin cases. You can comfortably fit 10 on a tray.
• Place on the low rack and cook for 15–18 minutes until cooked – they should spring back into shape when pressed.
• Place on a cooling rack to cool. If you are using silicon muffin cases, wait until they are cool, then carefully pull away at the sides of the case. Once clear all the way around, turn upside down and the cake should pop out.

Carrot Cake
Muffins with Vanilla Icing

MAKES 10–18

- Preheat the halogen oven using the preheat setting or set to 200°C.
- Cream the butter and sugar together until pale and fluffy.
- Add the eggs a little at a time and continue to beat well.
- Sift the flour and fold into the mixture gently.
- When thoroughly mixed, add the cinnamon, coriander, carrot and coconut and combine well.
- Place in cupcake or muffin cases on a muffin/cupcake tray. I use silicon muffin cases and place them on the halogen baking trays that come with the accessory packs. You can comfortably fit 10 on a tray.
- Place on the low rack and cook for 15–18 minutes. The cakes should be firm and spring back when touched.
- Place on a cooling rack to cool. If you are using silicon muffin cases, wait until they are cool and then carefully pull away at the sides of the case. Once clear all the way around, turn upside down and the cake should pop out.
- While the cakes are cooling, prepare the icing. Beat the butter and cream cheese together until soft. Gradually add the icing sugar and vanilla essence and beat until you reach the desired consistency – it should be glossy, thick and lump free. The best way of testing to see if you have added enough icing sugar is to taste it. It should taste sweet and creamy but not too buttery.
- Place the icing into an icing bag and fold down the ends to secure. Start in the centre of the cooled cakes and spiral outwards, covering the whole cake top and gently overlapping to avoid gaps. Finish with a sprinkle of cinnamon and you are ready to serve.

175g butter
175g brown sugar
3 eggs, beaten
175g self-raising flour
2 teaspoons cinnamon
1 teaspoon ground coriander
1 carrot, grated
50g desiccated coconut

Vanilla Icing
50g butter
100g cream cheese
200–275g icing sugar
1 teaspoon vanilla essence or paste
Cinnamon to sprinkle

Blueberry Muffins

MAKES 8–15

175g golden sugar
2 eggs, beaten
250ml natural yoghurt
1 teaspoon vanilla
  extract
300g self-raising flour
175g blueberries

SUITABLE FOR VEGETARIANS

- Preheat the halogen oven using the preheat setting or set the temperature to 190°C.
- Beat the sugar and eggs together until fluffy. Add the yoghurt and vanilla extract and beat again.
- Sift the flour into the mixture and carefully fold into the mix. When thoroughly mixed, add the blueberries.
- Place in cupcake or muffin cases in a muffin/cupcake tray. I have not been able to find a round muffin tray so I use silicon muffin cases and place them on the halogen baking trays that come with the accessory packs. You can comfortably fit 10 on a tray.
- Place on the low rack and cook for 12–18 minutes. The cakes should be firm and spring back when touched.
- Place on a cooling rack to cool. If you are using silicon muffin cases, wait until they are cool, then carefully pull away at the sides of the case. Once clear all the way around, turn upside down and the cake should pop out.

Orange Cupcakes

- Preheat the halogen oven using the preheat setting or set to 200°C.
- In a bowl combine the flour, sugar and cinnamon.
- Melt the butter and mix with the milk, orange extract, zest and egg. Combine well before mixing with the dry ingredients. Mix thoroughly.
- Place in cupcake or muffin cases in a muffin/cupcake tray. I use silicon muffin cases and place them on the halogen baking trays that come with the accessory packs. You can comfortably fit 10 on a tray.
- Place on the low rack and cook for 15–18 minutes. The cakes should be firm and spring back when touched.
- Place on a cooling rack to cool. If you are using silicon muffin cases, wait until they are cool, then carefully pull away at the sides of the case. Once clear all the way around, turn upside down and the cake should pop out.
- While the cakes are cooling, prepare the icing. Beat the butter and cream cheese together until soft. Gradually add the icing sugar and orange essence and beat until you reach the desired consistency – it should be glossy, thick and lump free. The best way of testing to see if you have added enough icing sugar is to taste it. It should taste sweet and creamy but not too buttery.
- Place the icing into an icing bag and fold down the ends to secure. Start in the centre of the cooled cakes and spiral outwards, covering the whole of the cake top and gently overlapping to avoid gaps. Finish with a few pieces of candied orange and you are ready to serve.

MAKES 10–15

120g self-raising flour
140g sugar
2 teaspoons cinnamon
40g butter
120ml full fat milk or buttermilk
1 teaspoon orange extract
Zest of 1 orange
1 egg

Orange Icing
50g butter
100g cream cheese
200–275g icing sugar
1 teaspoon orange essence
Candied orange pieces to finish

SUITABLE FOR VEGETARIANS

MAKES 8–15

175g butter
175g sugar
3 eggs, beaten
175g self-raising flour
2 teaspoons vanilla
  extract
1 small bar of dark
  chocolate

SUITABLE FOR VEGETARIANS

Vanilla Cupcakes with Chocolate Centre

- Preheat the halogen oven using the preheat setting or set to 200°C.
- Cream the butter and sugar together until pale and fluffy.
- Add the eggs a little at a time and continue to beat well.
- Sift the flour and gently fold into the mixture.
- When thoroughly mixed, add the vanilla extract and combine.
- I have not been able to find a round muffin tray so I use silicon muffin cases and place them on the halogen baking trays that come with the accessory packs. You can comfortably fit 10 on a tray. This mixture should make 8–15 cakes depending on their size.
- Place half the mixture in each of the cupcake or muffin cases. Make a small indent in the middle and add a square or two of chocolate. Add the remaining cake mixture over the top ensuring the chocolate is well covered and remains in the middle of the cake mix.
- Place on the low rack and cook for 14–18 minutes. The cakes should be firm and spring back when touched.
- Place on a cooling rack to cool. If you are using silicon muffin cases, wait until they are cool and then carefully pull away at the sides of the case. Once clear all the way around, turn upside down and the cake should pop out.

Coffee and Walnut Cupcakes

MAKES 10–18

- Preheat the halogen oven using the preheat setting or set to 200°C.
- Mix the instant coffee with the boiling water and leave to one side.
- Cream the butter and sugar together until pale and fluffy.
- Add the eggs a little at a time and continue to beat well. Add the coffee mixture and the chopped walnuts and stir well.
- Sift the flour and fold into the mixture gently until thoroughly combined.
- Place in silicon cupcake or muffin cases and stand on a tray. You can comfortably fit 10 on a tray.
- Place on the low rack and cook for 12–18 minutes. The cakes should be firm and spring back when touched.
- Place on a cooling rack to cool. If you are using silicon muffin cases, wait until they are cool, then carefully pull away at the sides of the case. Once clear all the way around, turn upside down and the cake should pop out.
- While the cakes are cooling, prepare the butter icing. Beat the butter until soft. Gradually add the icing sugar and coffee essence. Add a few drops of water at a time until you reach the desired consistency – it should be glossy, thick and lump free. The best way of testing to see if you have added enough icing sugar is to taste it. It should taste sweet and creamy but not too buttery.
- Place the icing in an icing bag and, starting from the centre, evenly coat the top of each cupcake. Finish with a few walnuts to decorate.

2 tablespoons instant coffee
30ml boiling water
175g butter
175g sugar
3 eggs, beaten
40g walnuts, finely chopped
175g self-raising flour

Coffee Icing
75g butter
150–175g icing sugar
1 teaspoon coffee essence
Drizzle of water
Walnuts to decorate

SUITABLE FOR VEGETARIANS

MAKES 10–18

175g butter
175g brown sugar
3 eggs, beaten
175g self-raising flour
2 or 3 food colourings
   or natural colourings
   such as cocoa,
   raspberries, vanilla
   essence

Icing
50g butter
100g cream cheese
200–275g icing sugar

SUITABLE FOR VEGETARIANS

Magic Rainbow Cupcakes

My son is fascinated with these cupcakes – he has now mastered the art of creating them himself, though I have to restrict him to only 2 or 3 colours or he would have a never ending mismatch going on. If you are not keen on using colours in your cakes, you can achieve the same effect using chocolate, raspberry and vanilla.

- Preheat the halogen oven using the preheat setting or set to 200°C.
- Cream the butter and sugar together until pale and fluffy.
- Add the eggs a little at a time and continue to beat well.
- Sift the flour and fold into the mixture gently. Ensure it is combined well.
- Place the mixture in two or three bowls, depending on how many colours you want to create. In each bowl, add your desired colour either by using a food colouring or naturally, for example you could use cocoa in one, raspberries in the other and vanilla essence in the plain one.
- I have not been able to find a round muffin/cupcake tray so I use silicon muffin cases and place them on the halogen baking trays that come with the accessory packs. You can comfortably fit 10 on a tray. This mixture should make 10–18 cakes depending on their size.
- Place random dollops of each colour in each cupcake case to create an uneven marble effect. Once complete, place on the low rack and cook for 14–18 minutes. The cakes should be firm and spring back when touched.

- Place on a cooling rack to cool. If you are using silicon muffin cases, wait until cool, then carefully pull away at the sides of the case. Once clear all the way around, turn upside down and the cake should pop out.
- While the cakes are cooling, prepare the icing. Beat the butter and cream cheese together until soft. Gradually add the icing sugar and beat until you reach the desired consistency – it should be glossy, thick and lump free. The best way of testing to see if you have added enough icing sugar is to taste it. It should taste sweet and creamy but not too buttery. If you want to create multicoloured icing, again, place the icing in two or three bowls and add your colouring before icing. This can be time consuming if you are using an icing bag as you will need to wash it out between each use. Another option would be to use one colour icing and decorate with multicoloured decorations.
- When ready, place the icing into an icing bag and fold down the ends to secure. Start in the centre of the cooled cakes and spiral outwards, covering the whole of the cake top and gently overlapping to avoid gaps. Finish with a sprinkle of decorations such as hundreds and thousands and you are ready to serve.

Cappuccino Cupcakes

MAKES 10–18

175g butter
175g sugar
3 eggs, beaten
175g self-raising flour
2–4 teaspoons coffee
essence, depending
on desired strength

Icing
50g butter
100g cream cheese
200–275g icing sugar
1 teaspoon vanilla
essence or paste
Cocoa to sprinkle

SUITABLE FOR VEGETARIANS

- Preheat the halogen oven using the preheat setting or set to 200°C.
- Cream the butter and sugar together until pale and fluffy.
- Add the eggs a little at a time and continue to beat well.
- Sift the flour and fold into the mixture gently.
- When well mixed, add the coffee essence and combine.
- Place in cupcake or muffin cases in a muffin/cupcake tray. I have not been able to find a round muffin tray so I use silicon muffin cases and place them on the halogen baking trays that come with the accessory packs. You can comfortably fit 10 on the tray.
- Place on the low rack and cook for 12–18 minutes. The cakes should be firm and spring back when touched.
- Place on a cooling rack to cool. If you are using silicon muffin cases, wait until they are cool, then carefully pull away at the sides of the case. Once clear all the way around, turn upside down and the cake should pop out.
- While the cakes are cooling, prepare the icing. Beat the butter and cream cheese together until soft. Gradually add the icing sugar and vanilla essence and beat until you reach the desired consistency – it should be glossy, thick and lump free. The best way of testing to see if you have added enough icing sugar is to taste it. It should taste sweet and creamy but not too buttery.
- Place the icing into an icing bag and fold down the ends to secure. Start in the centre of the cake and spiral outwards, covering the whole of the cake top and gently overlapping to avoid gaps. Finish with a sprinkle of cocoa to give a cappuccino effect, and you are ready to serve.

Mum's Lemon Curd Cupcakes

This is one of my mum's favourite recipes. The cupcakes are ideal for packed lunches, but beware, they might not last that long – they are yummy eaten warm!

- Preheat the halogen oven using the preheat setting or set to 200°C.
- Cream the butter and sugar together until pale and fluffy.
- Add the eggs a little at a time and continue to beat well.
- Sift the flour and baking powder and fold into the mixture gently.
- When thoroughly mixed, roughly fold in the sultanas and lemon curd. Don't over fold as you want the lemon curd to make a ripple effect.
- Place in cupcake or muffin cases in a muffin/cupcake tray. I have not been able to find a round muffin tray so I use silicon muffin cases and place them on the halogen baking trays that come with the accessory packs. You can comfortably fit 10 on the tray.
- Place on the low rack and cook for 12–18 minutes. The cakes should be firm and spring back when touched.
- While the cakes are cooking, juice and zest 1 lemon and mix together.
- Pour a little over each hot cake and finish with a sprinkle of sugar.
- If you are using silicon muffin cases, wait until they are cool, then carefully pull away at the sides of the case. Once clear all the way around, turn upside down and the cake should pop out.

MAKES 8–15

175g butter
150g sugar
3 large eggs, beaten
175g self-raising flour
1 teaspoon baking powder
125g sultanas
2 tablespoons lemon curd
Zest and juice of 1 lemon for topping
100g sugar for topping

SUITABLE FOR VEGETARIANS

Chocolate Chip Cupcakes with Vanilla Icing

8–15

50g cocoa
15ml boiling water
175g butter
175g sugar
3 eggs, beaten
175g self-raising flour
50g plain chocolate
 chips

Icing
50g butter
100g cream cheese
200–275g icing sugar
1 teaspoon vanilla
 essence or paste
Chocolate chips or
 grated chocolate to
 sprinkle

SUITABLE FOR VEGETARIANS

- Preheat the halogen oven using the preheat setting or set to 200°C.
- Mix the cocoa with the hot water and leave to one side.
- Cream the butter and sugar together until pale and fluffy.
- Add the eggs a little at a time and continue to beat well.
- Sift the flour and fold into the mixture gently.
- When thoroughly mixed, add the cocoa mixture and chocolate chips and combine.
- Place in cupcake or muffin cases in a muffin/cupcake tray. I have not been able to find a round muffin tray so I use silicon muffin cases and place them on the halogen baking trays that come with the accessory packs. You can comfortably fit 10 on the tray. This mixture should make 8–15 cakes depending on their size.
- Place on the low rack and cook for 12–18 minutes. The cakes should be firm and spring back when touched.
- Place on a cooling rack to cool. If you are using silicon muffin cases, wait until they are cool, then carefully pull away at the sides of the case. Once clear all the way around, turn upside down and the cake should pop out.

- While the cakes are cooling, prepare the icing. Beat the butter and cream cheese together until soft. Gradually add the icing sugar and vanilla essence and beat until you reach the desired consistency – it should be glossy, thick and lump free. The best way of testing to see if you have added enough icing sugar is to taste it. It should taste sweet and creamy but not too buttery.
- Place the icing into an icing bag and fold down the ends to secure. Start in the centre of the cake and spiral outwards, covering the whole of the cake top and gently overlapping to avoid gaps. Finish with a sprinkle of chocolate chips or grated chocolate and you are ready to serve.

Sugar, Spice and All Things Nice – Great Cakes and Fancies

'I am not a glutton – I'm an explorer of food'

– Erma Bombeck

I have always loved baking cakes and have ambitions to run my own tea room, but my family have not always been talented bakers. My Nan, bless her, was hopeless and would often have us in stitches with her culinary creations. One side of her cakes would be three or four inches high – the other side, a mere inch. Her Christmas cakes resembled ski slopes with the Christmas decorations hanging on for dear life but, truly, I would not have changed a thing.

It was important to me to master the art of baking cakes in the halogen oven. Online forums and comments from halogen users seem to indicate that there is a fear of making cakes. I truly believe it is due to people setting the temperature too high. The halogen is just like a very efficient conventional fan oven for which when baking traditional or old recipes you would turn the temperature down by 10–20°C. Use the halogen as you would your own conventional oven – don't be tempted to increase the temperature in order to speed things up as that will result in a burnt top and soggy middle and, let's be honest, none of us likes that!

Remember, your halogen's glass bowl allows you full sight of your cakes so there is no reason to be worried. If it looks as though it is browning too quickly, either cover securely with foil or, as I do, turn the temperature down slightly or add an extension ring.

I cannot stress enough that baking is never exact – I can bake the same cake and sometimes it takes a little longer to cook or comes out slightly differently. Much depends on mood, equipment used and your ingredients. As I am constantly changing recipes and literally just throw my ingredients in the bowl when baking, I thought it would be interesting to test a packet cake mix. I was embarrassed to have to buy it, but in the end I chose a lemon drizzle cake mix. I followed the recipe (other than adding some lemon zest, vanilla essence and a little fresh lemon juice!) and used a 1lb (0.5 kg) loaf tin (rather than their funny square cardboard box). The pack said 20 minutes at 180°C, preheated. The cake ended up taking 5 minutes longer as the centre was still a bit too soft, but it ended up pretty much on par with the pack instructions.

When I first started baking larger cakes in my halogen, I did have a problem with cooked tops but uncooked middles. The heat source comes from the top of the oven so it is understandable that the tops of cakes cook far quicker than the rest of the cake. I soon realised that I had to adjust the temperature, in some cases add the extension ring and I also established that the mixture should not be too wet. The problem normally arose when baking apple cakes or the more moist/wet cakes. To compensate for this, if you are using your favourite recipe, you may need to add more flour to make a firmer mix. Keep the temperature the same as when baking with your conventional oven to start with and see how you go. Some cakes are exactly the same; some may need adjustment – usually a little longer at lower temperatures, particularly larger cakes.

When making cakes use the best ingredients you can afford. Always sift the flour and beat the eggs where appropriate. A good food mixer makes easy work of cake making. I always use good quality cake tins and I have recently been converted to using cake liners. They are really cheap to buy: I think I pay 99p for 20 from our local discount store. They make cake making so easy and avoid the disaster of cakes sticking to the tins when you turn them out.

To test if your cake is done, feel the top first – a sponge cake should be firm and spring back to shape when pressed. A fruit cake or larger cake should have a firm top and is best tested with a skewer or clean knife which, when inserted into the centre of the cake, should come away clean. If there is cake mixture on the skewer or knife, it is still not cooked in the middle so will need more time. Fruit cakes often need to be cooked for longer on a lower temperature and timings can vary depending on the size of the cake and the ingredients used. I always leave the cake in the tin for 5 minutes once removed from the halogen before turning it out onto the cooling rack.

Banana and Chocolate Cake

125g butter

125g sugar

2 tablespoons honey

1 teaspoon vanilla
essence

2 eggs, beaten

1 ripe banana, mashed

175g self-raising flour

4 tablespoons cocoa

SUITABLE FOR VEGETARIANS

If your children are anything like mine, a banana with slightly browning skin is declared as gone off – even though the flesh is perfect. This cake is ideal for using up any 'brown' or ripe bananas. The result is a moist, yummy cake your family will adore – just don't mention the brown bananas! This should be baked in a loaf tin and can be sliced. Store in an airtight container and it will keep fresh for days.

- Preheat the halogen oven using the preheat setting or set the temperature to 190°C.
- Using your cake mixer, beat the butter and sugar together until light and fluffy. Add the honey, vanilla essence and beaten eggs and mix again.
- Add the banana, before adding the sifted dry ingredients. Combine well.
- Pour into a well greased or lined cake or loaf tin and bake on the low rack for 25–35 minutes, or until a skewer comes out clean when pushed into the centre of the cake.
- Remove from the halogen and leave to cool slightly before turning out onto a cooling rack.
- Decorate with melted chocolate or vanilla icing (see Chapter 5 for icing recipes).

Aunty's Dundee Cake

This wonderful cake is cooked on a low heat for almost 2 hours. Keep an eye on the top of the cake – sometimes, depending on halogen models (I have noticed a difference), the top may start to darken. If so, just cover securely with foil. Alternatively, you could opt to cook using the extension ring. This places the halogen element further away and can reduce browning, though you may have to extend the cooking time slightly.

- Place the dried fruit in a bowl and add the whisky or brandy. This gives the fruit a little time to absorb the alcohol. If you don't want to use alcohol, you can opt for orange juice.
- Preheat the halogen oven to 150°C.
- Using your cake mixer, combine the butter and brown sugar. Add the treacle and zest and mix well.
- Add the eggs, a little at a time, before sifting in the dry ingredients. Combine well. Now add the fruit including the liquid (if any).
- Stir well. Pour this into a very well greased or lined round cake tin. Press down gently to level out the top before adding the whole almonds to form a decorative/attractive pattern on top.
- Place your cake on the low rack and cook on the low heat for 1½ –2 hours. To test if the cake is cooked, insert a skewer into the middle of the cake. If it comes out clean, it is cooked.
- Remove from the oven and leave to cool for a few minutes before turning out onto a cooling rack.

350g mixed dried fruit
1–2 tablespoons whisky or brandy
175g butter
150g brown sugar
1 generous tablespoon dark treacle
Zest of 1 orange
Zest of 1 lemon
4 eggs, beaten
30g ground almonds
125g self-raising flour
125g plain flour
½ teaspoon baking powder
50g whole almonds

SUITABLE FOR VEGETARIANS

Healthy Fruit Cake

200g dates
300ml tea or water
175g self-raising flour
1 teaspoon baking
  powder
400g dried mixed fruit
Grated rind of 1
  orange
1 tablespoon orange
  juice
2 teaspoons mixed
  spice

SUITABLE FOR VEGETARIANS

I discovered this fruit cake recipe in my great aunt's recipe scrapbook. I don't know where she acquired it but it is a fatless, sugarless, eggless fruit cake and very simple to make.

- Preheat the halogen oven using the preheat setting or set the temperature to 170°C.
- Place the dates and tea or water into a saucepan and gently heat on your hob until the dates are soft. Remove the pan from the heat and mash to break up the dates.
- In a large mixing bowl sift the flour and baking powder. Add the mixed fruit, orange rind and orange juice and mix thoroughly.
- Add the date mixture and stir well.
- Spoon the mixture into a greased or lined 1lb (0.5kg) loaf or cake tin. Level the top. Place on the low rack in the halogen oven. Bake for 45 minutes. Then reduce the heat to 150°C and cook for a further 15–30 minutes until a skewer or knife inserted into the cake comes out clean.
- Turn out onto a cooling rack. Serve sliced.

Upside Down Blackberry and Apple Cake

Use a spring, loose-bottomed cake tin for this. It looks really impressive when turned out onto a nice cake plate or stand and sprinkled with sieved icing sugar. Delicious hot or cold.

- Preheat the halogen oven using the preheat setting or set the temperature to 190°C.
- Generously grease a cake tin with butter.
- Place the apple slices, blackberries and 1 tablespoon of sugar in the base of your cake tin.
- Beat the butter and sugar until light and fluffy. Add the eggs a little at a time, and then add the sifted flour. Once mixed, add the vanilla extract and cinnamon. Combine well.
- Place the cake mixture over the apple and blackberries. I use a silicon spatula as it clears the bowl and is easy to use. Smooth the surface gently but don't over fuss as you don't want to lift the fruit from the bottom.
- Place on the low rack and cook for 25–30 minutes, until the cake is cooked, firm and springs back to shape when touched.
- When ready to serve, place an upturned plate, slightly larger than the top of the cake, on the top of the cake tin. Flip over so that the cake tin is upside down on top of the plate, and allow the cake to drop down onto the plate. If you are using a spring cake tin, undo it, releasing the cake.
- Sprinkle with sifted icing sugar to decorate before serving hot or cold with a spoonful of cream or crème fraîche.

2–3 cooking apples, sliced
150g blackberries
1 tablespoon sugar
175g butter
175g sugar
3 eggs
175g self-raising flour, sifted
1 teaspoon vanilla extract
2 teaspoons ground cinnamon

SUITABLE FOR VEGETARIANS

Rich Chocolate and Date Cake

75g dark chocolate

2 tablespoons milk

75g sugar

110g butter

3 eggs, beaten

½ teaspoon vanilla
   essence

75g self-raising flour

30g rice flour

1 teaspoon baking
   powder

75g dates, chopped

SUITABLE FOR VEGETARIANS

A gorgeous cake for chocoholics. Don't overcook as you want it to be nice and moist, not dry.

- Melt the chocolate and stir in the milk – you can use a bain marie for this or your microwave.
- Beat the sugar and butter until light and fluffy.
- Add the chocolate before adding the eggs and vanilla essence
- Sift the dry ingredients and add to the mixture. Combine thoroughly before adding the chopped dates.
- Pour into a lined cake tin.
- Preheat the halogen oven using the preheat setting or set the temperature to 170°C.
- Bake on the low rack for 50 minutes to 1 hour before testing. It should be firm to the touch, spring back and a skewer placed into the cake should come out clean.
- Leave in the tin for 5 minutes before turning out onto a cooling rack.
- Serve sliced hot or cold – delicious!

Orange Cake

Another family favourite stolen from my Mum's scrapbook of recipes. I use orange essence. I would advise you buy the best you can afford as it does make a difference!

- Preheat the halogen oven using the preheat setting or turn the temperature to 180°C.
- Beat the butter and sugar together until creamy. Add the eggs, beat again and then add the flour, milk, orange essence and zest.
- Pour into a greased loaf tin. Place on the low rack and cook for 30–40 minutes, until firm and cooked.
- Turn out onto a cooling rack.
- Mix the orange juice and icing sugar together. Pour this over the cooled cake. You can also decorate with a few slices of candied orange peel.

150g butter
150g sugar
2 eggs
200g self-raising flour
2 tablespoons milk
1 teaspoon orange essence
Zest and juice of 1 orange
3 tablespoons icing sugar

SUITABLE FOR VEGETARIANS

½ teaspoon
   bicarbonate of soda
4 tablespoons milk
110g butter
110g moist brown
   sugar
175g black treacle or
   golden syrup
225g plain flour
10g ground ginger
1 teaspoon lemon
   rind, grated
1 egg

SUITABLE FOR VEGETARIANS

Aunty Ruth's Fabulous Dark Ginger Cake

When I was growing up, a visit to Aunty Ruth's house meant afternoon tea with delicious cakes and jelly and blancmange served in amazing animal shapes. Not really a surprise as she was a real animal lover. Her garden was full of wild birds and even a family of hedgehogs. She was a wonderful cook. Here is one of her great recipes – I hope you enjoy it.

- Preheat the halogen oven using the preheat setting or set the temperature to 150°C.
- Blend the bicarbonate of soda with 1 tablespoon of milk. Put the butter, sugar and treacle or syrup in a saucepan and heat until the butter has melted. Add the remaining milk and heat gently.
- Sieve the flour and ginger together in a bowl. Add the melted butter and syrup mixture, along with the milk and bicarbonate mixture, lemon rind and egg. Whisk until well combined.
- Thoroughly grease or line a cake tin (I use a 7in/18cm tin). Pour in the mixture and bake on the low rack for 1 hour 10 minutes to 1 hour 30 minutes. Test to see if it is cooked by gently pressing the centre of the cake – if there is no impression it is cooked.
- Leave in the tin until cool then turn onto a cooling rack.
- Serve iced or topped with sliced candied ginger.

Mocha Cake

If you love mocha, this cake is for you – finish with white icing and chocolate drizzle for a perfect afternoon tea cake.

- Beat the sugar and butter together until light and fluffy.
- Add the beaten eggs, milk, coffee essence and cocoa and combine well.
- Add the sifted flour and fold in until evenly combined.
- Place in a greased or lined cake tin.
- Preheat the halogen oven using the preheat setting or set the temperature to 180°C.
- Place on the low rack and cook for 45–50 minutes or until firm to the touch and a skewer inserted into the cake comes out clean.
- Once cooled, cover with white icing (mix the icing sugar and a few drops of water until you form an icing paste, thick enough to cover the cake) and finish with a drizzle of melted piped dark chocolate.

110g sugar
110g butter
2 eggs, beaten
1–2 tablespoons milk
1 level tablespoon coffee essence
1 heaped tablespoon cocoa
175g self-raising flour, sifted
150g icing sugar

SUITABLE FOR VEGETARIANS

Orange Coconut Cake

175g butter
175g sugar
Zest of 1 orange
3 eggs, separated
40ml orange juice
225g self-raising flour,
  sifted
1 teaspoon orange
  essence
50g desiccated
  coconut

SUITABLE FOR VEGETARIANS

This is a lovely cake. I found the recipe in an old scrapbook of recipes I bought on eBay. I hope you enjoy it!

• Cream the butter and sugar together until light and fluffy.
• Add the orange zest and the egg yolks and beat again.
• Stir in the orange juice gradually, alternating with spoonfuls of sifted flour. Once combined, add the orange essence and coconut.
• Whisk the egg whites until they form soft peaks and then carefully fold into the cake mixture.
• Once combined, place in a lined cake tin.
• Preheat the halogen oven using the preheat setting or set the temperature to 180°C.
• Place on the low rack and cook for 30 minutes.
• Remove from the oven and sprinkle with icing sugar while still warm.
• Place on a cooling rack. Store in an airtight container.

Fruit Scones

This is a basic, traditional recipe for scones. Use it as a base and omit the fruit if you prefer plain scones, or add some grated mature Cheddar and a pinch of paprika or cayenne pepper for a lovely savoury scone.

- Preheat the halogen oven using the preheat setting or set the temperature to 210°C.
- Sift the flour into a bowl. Add the butter and rub to form breadcrumbs. Add the sugar and dried fruit and combine well.
- Gradually add the milk to form a firm but not wet dough.
- Place this on a floured surface, and press out until 3–4cm thick. Cut with a pastry cutter and place on a greased baking tray. Brush with milk
- Bake for 10 minutes then place on a cooling rack.
- Serve with cream and jam for a traditional cream tea.

MAKES 8–10

200g self-raising flour
30g butter
30g sugar
125ml milk
50g raisins or mixed
   fruit (optional)

SUITABLE FOR VEGETARIANS

MAKES 6–8

225g self-raising flour
½ teaspoon baking
   powder
25g sugar
50g butter
100g blueberries
150ml natural yoghurt
1 teaspoon vanilla
   essence
Milk to glaze
A sprinkling of brown
   sugar

SUITABLE FOR VEGETARIANS

Blueberry Scones

This is a very light scone and is best eaten on the day it is made.

- Preheat the halogen oven using the preheat setting or set the temperature to 200°C.
- Sift the flour, baking powder and sugar into a bowl. Rub in the butter until it resembles breadcrumbs.
- Add the blueberries, yoghurt and vanilla essence and mix to form a dough.
- On a floured surface, roll out the dough into a thick sausage. Cut 2.5–5cm (1–2in) pieces and place these flat onto a greased or lined baking tray.
- Brush with milk and sprinkle over some brown sugar before placing on the low rack for 10–12 minutes.
- Place on a cooling rack before serving.

Variations
Omit the blueberries to make Plain Scones. Add 75g of dried mixed fruit to make Fruit Scones, or choose your own fabulous flavours.

Chocolate and Apple Cake

My favourite combination: chocolate and apple – yum! I found this recipe tucked away in one of my mum's scrapbooks. I have adapted it slightly to make a richer chocolate cake but you can cut back if you don't want the richness.

- Cream the butter and sugar together until light and fluffy.
- Add the egg and the milk and combine.
- Fold in the sifted flour and cocoa. This makes quite a loose batter.
- Place half the mixture in a greased cake tin. Cover with grated apple and finish with the remaining batter.
- Preheat the halogen oven using the preheat setting or set the temperature to 190°C.
- Place on the low rack and cook for 30–40 minutes until firm and a skewer comes out clean when inserted.
- Cool for 5 minutes before turning out onto a cooling rack.
- Once cool you can cover with icing.

110g butter
110g sugar
1 egg
60ml milk
225g self-raising flour, sifted
2 tablespoons cocoa, sifted
1–2 cooking apples, grated

SUITABLE FOR VEGETARIANS

225g butter
225g caster sugar
4 eggs, beaten
1 teaspoon vanilla
    extract (optional)
225g sifted self-raising
    flour
Raspberry jam

SUITABLE FOR VEGETARIANS

Victoria Sponge

This is a wonderful, traditional sponge, normally filled with raspberry jam and sprinkled with caster sugar, but feel free to adapt it to suit your own preferences. I love combining a butter cream filling with a nice sharp raspberry jam. I use vanilla extract in my sponge – force of habit and a passion for vanilla, but feel free to take this out if you want to stick to the traditional recipe.

- Beat the butter and sugar until light and fluffy. Add the eggs, a little at a time to avoid curdling. If it does curdle, just add a spoon of your sifted flour.
- Add the vanilla extract before folding in the sifted self-raising flour.
- Preheat the halogen oven using the preheat setting or set the temperature to 180°C.
- Divide the mixture into two greased, deep sponge tins.
- Place one on the low rack and bake for 20–25 minutes until firm but springs back when touched. (You can bake them both at the same time if you use an extension ring to increase the height of the oven, though the top sponge will cook faster than the bottom one and this could affect the finished result.)
- Place on a cooling rack to cool before filling with raspberry jam. Sprinkle sugar over the top to complete – delicious!

Fatless Sponge

My mum makes a mean fatless sponge, especially when she uses her homemade raspberry jam to fill it … yum! I would strongly advise using a good quality jam rather than a very sickly, sweet one – you want to have the sharp taste of the raspberries. I have pinched her recipe to share with you, so go on, and enjoy a guilt-free pleasure!

3 eggs, separated
225g sugar (ideally
  caster sugar)
75ml warm water
150g self-raising flour
Raspberry jam to fill

SUITABLE FOR VEGETARIANS

- Preheat the halogen oven using the preheat setting or set the temperature to 180°C. Grease two deep sponge tins with butter. Sprinkle on a little flour and ensure the butter is coated. This forms a perfect non-stick base.
- Mix the egg yolks and sugar together, adding the warm water a little at a time. This normally takes about 10 minutes to ensure a light and fluffy texture.
- Sift the flour and gently add a little at a time into the egg and sugar mix – **don't whisk**.
- In a clean bowl, whisk the egg whites until firm, and then very gently fold into the cake mixture.
- Divide the mixture into the two greased sponge tins. Place one on the low rack and bake for 20–25 minutes until it is firm but springs back when touched. (You can bake them both at the same time if you use an extension ring to increase the height of the oven, though the top sponge will cook faster than the bottom one and this could affect the finished result.)
- Place on a cooling rack to cool before filling with raspberry jam. Sprinkle sugar over the top to complete – delicious!

175g butter
175g sugar
3 eggs, beaten
200g self-raising flour
Zest and juice of 2
  lemons

Icing
50g butter
100g cream cheese
300g icing sugar
Zest of 1 lemon

SUITABLE FOR VEGETARIANS

Lemon Cream Sponge

This is a lovely sponge with a lemon creamy filling. If you prefer, you can also put the lemon cream all over the cake and decorate with lemon candied slices, for a really decadent gâteau.

- Preheat the halogen oven using the preheat setting or set to 200°C.
- Cream the butter and sugar together until pale and fluffy.
- Add the eggs a little at a time and continue to beat well.
- Sift the flour and fold into the mixture gently.
- When thoroughly mixed, add the lemon juice and zest and combine. For an extra lemon tang you could add a little lemon essence, but buy a good quality one or it can taste too artificial.
- Place in two greased sponge tins.
- Turn the halogen oven on to 150°C, with the fan on full (if applicable).
- If you have an extension ring, you could cook the sponges together. However, if you don't have one I would advise cooking them on the low rack one at a time. If you use an extension ring, place one on the low rack and one on the high rack but keep an eye on the top one as you may want to swap them over halfway through cooking or the top may be cooked a few minutes before the lower one.
- Bake for 25–35 minutes until firm to touch and the cake has pulled away slightly from the edges of the tin.

• While the cakes are cooling, prepare the icing. Beat
the butter and cream cheese together until soft.
Gradually add the icing sugar and lemon zest and
beat until you reach the desired consistency – it
should be glossy, thick and lump free. The best way of
testing to see if you have added enough icing sugar is
to taste it. It should taste sweet and creamy but not
too buttery.

• Spread on one of the sponges and sandwich together.
For an extra touch of lemon, you could spread with
lemon curd as well as the butter icing before
sandwiching together. If you prefer, you can place
icing on the top or around the sides, or even all over.
Finish with a couple of slices of lemon to garnish.

220ml stewed tea
300g mixed dried fruit
125g butter (if vegan,
   use dairy-free
   margarine)
125g brown sugar
2 teaspoons cinnamon
1 teaspoon allspice
40g dried apple rings
250g self-raising flour

SUITABLE FOR VEGETARIANS

Boiled Fruit and Tea Loaf

This is an old recipe which I have adapted slightly. The fruit and the tea are ideally left overnight so the fruits absorb the liquid and the result is a moist loaf.

- Put the kettle on and make 200ml of tea (without milk!) and leave to stew for 5 minutes.
- Meanwhile, in a large saucepan, add the dried fruit, butter and sugar. Finally, add the tea when ready.
- Place on a moderate heat and gently allow the butter to melt and the sugar to dissolve. Keep stirring, as you don't want it to stick or burn. Once melted, add the spices. Boil for 1 minute then remove from the heat.
- Using sharp scissors snip the apple rings into pieces and drop into the saucepan. Stir well and leave until cold, or overnight if you prefer.
- Once cooled and absorbed, sift in the flour and stir well until thoroughly combined.
- Preheat the halogen oven using the preheat setting or set to 180°C.
- Thoroughly grease or line your loaf tin and pour in the mixture. I now use cake liners as they are so easy and worry free.
- Place on the low rack and cook for 20 minutes. Check the cake and if the top is getting too dark, cover with some brown paper, but make sure it is secure without restricting the cake, or add extension ring.
- Turn down to 160°C and cook for another 25–35 minutes, or until a skewer, when inserted into the centre of the cake, comes out clean.
- Leave to cool in the cake tin before turning out onto a cooling rack.

Pineapple Upside-Down Cake

A traditional family favourite that can be served as a pudding or a cake.

- In your food mixer, mix 175g butter and 175g sugar until golden and creamy. Gradually add the eggs and combine well.
- Fold in the sifted flour and, once combined thoroughly, add the vanilla essence. Leave to one side.
- Preheat the halogen oven using the preheat setting or set the temperature to 180°C.
- Place 50g butter, 50g brown sugar and the golden syrup in an ovenproof bowl and, using the preheat temperature, melt the butter, but do not let it burn.
- Grease or line an ovenproof dish or cake tin thoroughly. Place a small amount of the butter/sugar mixture into the dish, then place the pineapple rings in the bottom with the cherries in the middle of the rings. Pour on the remaining melted butter/sugar.
- Carefully spoon on the sponge mix to cover the pineapple rings. Once completely covered, carefully smooth over the surface.
- Place on the low rack and cook until the sponge has risen, is golden and springs back into shape when touched – this should take between 25 and 30 minutes.
- Remove from the oven. Place a plate or serving dish over the top of the cake dish and flip over so the cake sits on the plate, upside down, pineapple facing upwards.
- Serve with a dollop of crème fraîche.

175g butter
175g sugar
3 eggs, beaten
175g self-raising flour, sifted
1 teaspoon vanilla essence
50g butter
50g brown sugar
2 tablespoons golden syrup
Pineapple rings
3 glace cherries, halved
Crème fraîche to serve

SUITABLE FOR VEGETARIANS

Death by Chocolate Orange

75g cocoa
¾ teaspoon
   bicarbonate of soda
100ml boiling water
100ml orange juice
300g golden sugar
4 eggs
1 teaspoon vanilla
   paste
1 teaspoon orange
   essence
180ml light olive oil
200g self-raising flour

Icing

200g dark chocolate
   (70% cocoa),
   broken into pieces
40g unsalted butter
100ml milk
50g cocoa
1 orange essence
2 tablespoons honey

SUITABLE FOR VEGETARIANS

This is my son's favourite cake. I used to make it in my normal oven, but I have since swapped to the halogen and it works well. It is a very rich chocolate orange cake with a thick, rich fudge-like icing.

• Mix the cocoa and bicarbonate of soda with the boiling water. Once dissolved well, add the orange juice and leave to one side.
• Grease and/or line two sponge tins.
• Beat the sugar and eggs together until light and creamy. Add the vanilla paste, orange essence and olive oil and continue beating well.
• Add the flour, followed by the cocoa solution. You can continue to beat this – you don't need to fold. This will form a batter the consistency of double cream.
• Pour the batter into the two sponge tins.
• Turn the halogen oven on to 170°C, with fan on full (if applicable).
• If you have an extension ring, you could cook the sponges together. However, if you don't have one I would advise cooking them on the low rack one at a time. If you use an extension ring, place one on the low rack and one on the high rack but keep an eye on the top one as you may want to swap them over halfway through cooking or the top may cook a few minutes before the lower one.
• Bake for 20–30 minutes until firm to touch and the cake has pulled away slightly from the edges of the tin.

- Once cool, place on a cooling rack while you make the icing.
- In a bain marie (or bowl placed over a saucepan), add all the icing ingredients and allow them to melt and blend together to form a chocolate sauce. Stir well.
- Place one sponge, flat side up, on your serving plate or cake stand. Spread half the icing mix onto the sponge and place the remaining sponge over the top to form a sandwich. Use the remaining icing to cover the top of the sponge. It will set so don't worry if it drips down the sides of the cake. Enjoy!

Candied Fruit and Nut Cake

This is a light fruit cake, using candied fruit alongside some dried fruit favourites.

125g sugar
125g butter
3 eggs
1 teaspoon vanilla
essence
225g self-raising flour
2 teaspoons baking
powder
1 teaspoon mixed
spice
75g dried figs
75g apricots
50g glace cherries
50g candied pineapple
25g candied peel
50g dates
100g raisins
75g almonds, chopped
50g hazelnuts,
chopped

SUITABLE FOR VEGETARIANS

- In a food mixer or mixing bowl combine the sugar and butter together until light and fluffy. Beat the eggs with the vanilla essence before adding to the creamed mixture.
- Sift the dry ingredients and fold into the cake mixture until thoroughly combined.
- Finely chop the dried and candied fruit and add with the nuts to the cake mixture. Stir well.
- Preheat the halogen oven using the preheat setting or set the temperature to 175°C.
- Pour into a lined cake or loaf tin. Place on the low rack and cook for 1 hour 30 minutes until a skewer inserted into the cake comes out clean. Serve sliced with a cup of tea!

Madeira Cake

A traditional favourite everyone enjoys.

- Beat the butter and sugar together until light, fluffy and creamy. Add the egg gradually. If it starts to curdle, add a little flour to compensate.
- Add the vanilla extract and the milk (or brandy) and combine before adding the sifted flours and lemon zest. Stir well until evenly combined.
- Preheat the halogen oven using the preheat setting or set the temperature to 170°C.
- Line a cake tin and pour in the mixture. Place on the low rack and cook for 30 minutes. Test to see if it is cooked by inserting a skewer or sharp knife into the cake. If it comes out clean, it is cooked; if not, continue to cook for another 10 minutes and test again.
- Once cooked, leave in the cake tin for at least 5 minutes before turning out onto a cooling rack.
- Once cooled, sprinkle with icing sugar or decorate with candied lemon peel.

175g butter
175g sugar
3 eggs, beaten
1 teaspoon vanilla extract
20ml milk (or 30ml brandy if you prefer)
175g self-raising flour, sifted
50g cornflour, sifted
Zest of 1 lemon

SUITABLE FOR VEGETARIANS

225g butter

225g sugar

4 eggs

1 teaspoon vanilla
essence

3–4 drops almond
essence

175g self-raising flour

50g cornflour

½ teaspoon baking
powder

110g ground almonds

200g glace cherries,
chopped

SUITABLE FOR VEGETARIANS

Mum's Cherry Cake

I must confess that as a child I was never very keen on glace cherries so I would end up with a mutilated cake, eating the sponge and leaving a trail of chopped cherries all around my plate. I can't say my tastes have improved dramatically but I do tolerate the cherries more now. This cake has been included as it is a family favourite and perfect with afternoon tea. As with all deeper cakes baked in the halogen, you will need to cook on a lower heat than normal to avoid a burnt top and soggy middle. If the top seems to be getting too dark, you can cover the tin securely with tin foil or add an extension ring (lifting the element further away from the top of the cake).

- In a bowl, cream the butter and sugar together until light and fluffy – I use a food mixer for this.
- Beat the eggs in a jug or bowl and then add the vanilla and almond essence. Gradually add this to the butter and sugar mixture. If it starts to look as though it will curdle, add a spoonful or two of sifted flour.
- Once mixed, add the sifted flour, cornflour and baking powder. Carefully fold in, making sure it is thoroughly combined.
- Finally add the ground almonds and the cherries, again ensuring they are evenly distributed.
- Preheat the halogen oven using the preheat setting or set the temperature to 170°C.
- Line a cake tin – I prefer to use cake liners as they make life so much easier. Pour in the mixture and carefully smooth down the top ensuring it is evenly spread.
- Place on the low rack and cook for 1 hour, checking after 30–40 minutes to see if it is getting too dark on top. If it is, cover with foil or add the extension ring.

- After 1 hour, turn the temperature down to 150°C and cook for another 15–30 minutes or until the cake is cooked.
- Once cooked, turn out onto a cooling rack.
- Store in an airtight container.

Honey and Ginger Cake

The old recipes are the best – this is delicious.

- Place the butter, sugar and honey in a saucepan and heat gently until melted and combined. Take off the heat and add the beaten eggs.
- In a bowl, sift the flour and add the ginger, baking powder and chopped dates.
- Pour the melted mixture into the dry mixture and combine well.
- Place this in a greased or lined cake tin – I use a loaf tin. Spread gently to even out the top of the cake.
- Preheat the halogen oven using the preheat setting or set the temperature to 180°C.
- Place on the low rack and cook for 25–30 minutes until cooked (use a skewer to test).
- Leave in the cake tin for 5 minutes before turning out onto a cooling rack. Slice when cool.

110g butter
110g brown sugar
4 tablespoons runny honey
2 eggs, beaten
225g self-raising flour
1 tablespoon ground ginger
½ teaspoon baking powder
30g dates, finely chopped

SUITABLE FOR VEGETARIANS

Fruity Carrot Cake

3 carrots, grated
250g sugar
330ml water
75g dates, chopped
100g raisins or
    currants
125g butter or vegan
    spread
2 teaspoons cinnamon
1 teaspoon ground
    coriander
500g self-raising flour
75g chopped nuts
1 teaspoon baking
    powder
Zest of ½ a lemon

SUITABLE FOR VEGETARIANS
AND VEGANS

This is a really simple cake to make – it is all done in a saucepan! It is also eggless so suitable for vegans if you swap the butter for vegan spread. Very moist and delicious – worth giving it a go!

- Place the carrots, sugar, water and dried fruit in a saucepan and bring to the boil for about 2–3 minutes.
- Add the butter or vegan spread, cinnamon and ground coriander. Remove from the heat and allow to cool completely (this is very important!).
- Once completely cooled, sift in the flour and baking powder. Add the nuts and lemon zest and combine well. It may look a bit of a mess but, believe me, it will be worth it.
- Preheat the halogen oven using the preheat setting or set the temperature to 180°C.
- Place the cake mixture into a lined cake tin. Place on the low rack and cook for 30 minutes. Turn the temperature down to 150°C and cook for a further 30 minutes or until the cake is cooked. To test, place a clean knife or skewer into the centre of the cake – when it comes out clean it is cooked.
- Turn out onto a cooling rack.
- Serve as it is or for extra decadence top with icing (see Chapter 5 for ideas). Alternatively, I love Delia's Mascarpone, Fromage Frais and Cinnamon Icing: combine 150g mascarpone, 100g fromage frais, 1 heaped teaspoon cinnamon and 1 rounded teaspoon caster sugar. Beat until fluffy. Cover and chill for at least 1 hour before adding to the cake.

Mary's Lemon Cake

Yet another family scrapbook find. I'm not sure who Mary is, but this is a really lovely recipe. As with any long-cook cakes, you will need to keep an eye on the top to make sure it does not get too brown. It would traditionally be cooked in a conventional oven at 170°C, but I cook it at 150–160°C in the halogen and it works well, avoiding the top cooking faster than the middle.

- Sift the flour into a bowl and rub in the butter to form breadcrumbs.
- Add the sugar, cherries, sultanas and lemon zest. Combine well.
- In a jug, beat the eggs and add the milk, lemon, and vanilla essence. Add this to the dry mixture and combine well. This is quite a runny batter hence the long cook time.
- Pour into a lined loaf tin.
- Preheat the halogen oven using the preheat setting or set the temperature to about 155°C. 160°C is fine but keep an eye on it as towards the end of the bake you may want to turn it down slightly.
- Bake on the low rack for 1 hour. Keep an eye on it through the glass bowl to see if it looks cooked – it can sometimes take up to 1 hour 20 minutes, depending on the mixture. When you are confident, use a skewer to test.
- Once cooked, remove from the oven and leave to cool for 5 minutes before turning out onto a cooling rack.
- Serve sliced with a handful of fresh raspberries – delicious!

325g self-raising flour
110g butter
175g soft brown sugar
50g glace cherries, chopped
110g sultanas
Zest of 2 lemons
2 eggs
175ml milk
Juice of 1 lemon
1 teaspoon vanilla essence

SUITABLE FOR VEGETARIANS

110g butter
110g sugar
1 egg, beaten
3 ripe bananas,
   mashed
½ teaspoon
   bicarbonate of soda
2 tablespoons milk
225g self-raising flour,
   sifted

SUITABLE FOR VEGETARIANS

Banana Cake

Use up those brown bananas with this delicious cake. Very simple and moist – yummy!

- Cream the butter and sugar together until light and fluffy.
- Add the beaten egg and mashed bananas and combine well.
- Dissolve the bicarbonate of soda in the milk and add this to the banana mixture.
- Fold in the sifted flour until thoroughly combined.
- Preheat the halogen oven using the preheat setting or set the temperature to 180°C.
- Place the mixture in a lined or greased baking tin (I use a loaf tin) and bake on the low rack for 25–30 minutes until cooked.
- Leave to cool in the tin before turning out onto a cooling rack.

Spicy Apple Cake

This is a lovely apple cake that actually improves if left for a couple of days, making it perfect for packed lunches. I adore apple cake so I am always interested to discover new ideas and recipes. This gem was found in my great aunt's recipe scrapbook.

- Cream the butter and the sugar until light and fluffy.
- Add the eggs a little at a time. Then add the walnuts and sultanas.
- Sift in the flour, baking powder and mixed spice and combine well before adding the cooked apples.
- Pour into a lined cake tin and smooth to level off.
- Preheat the halogen oven using the preheat setting or set the temperature to 180°C.
- Place on the low rack and cook for 45 minutes. Touch the top to see if it is cooked. If not, turn the heat down to 160°C and cook for a further 10–20 minutes until a skewer inserted into the cake comes out clean (though remember the apples will make the skewer wet, but this looks very different from uncooked cake).
- Once cooked, leave in the tin for 5 minutes before turning out onto a cooling rack.
- Store in an airtight container until needed.

175g butter
175g sugar
3 eggs, well beaten
50g walnuts, chopped
50g sultanas
225g plain flour
1 teaspoon baking powder
1–2 teaspoons mixed spice
1½ cups of cooked apples, pureed (unsweetened)

SUITABLE FOR VEGETARIANS

The Coffee Break – Dunkable Biscuits and Treats

'As you bake, so shall you brew'

– Proverb, 16th Century

We are so used to shop-bought biscuits we have forgotten the delight and yumminess of homemade. Days just seem too short and time too precious to spend making biscuits, but really, I urge you to try at least some of these recipes. Cookies just aren't the same when shop-bought – there is nothing quite as nice as nibbling away on a warm cookie straight from the oven. Those dry, tasteless cookies just cannot compete.

The halogen oven is perfectly capable of baking delicious cakes and biscuits. Don't be tempted to cook them on too high a heat. If you are following your favourite recipe which you would usually bake in your conventional oven, you may need to adjust the timings or temperature slightly but not too much. Some experts suggest a 10% reduction on temperature and time. The following recipes have been tested in my halogen oven. Some machines vary so keep a watch ready to adjust timings where necessary.

When baking biscuits, remember that they often harden when cool so it is advisable to remove them from the oven when they are slightly soft rather than wait for them to harden whilst cooking – which would result in rock hard biscuits you could break your teeth on!

As with all cake and biscuit recipes, you can use the extension ring to lift the element away from the top of the food. This can prevent the cakes or biscuits from browning too quickly. I include a note about this in recipes where I personally use this technique. I prefer to cook biscuits on the non-stick browning tray (available from halogen accessory dealers or Amazon).

Melting Moments

MAKES 8–12 DEPENDING ON SIZE

225g butter
50g icing sugar
½ teaspoon vanilla
  essence
175g self-raising flour,
  sifted
50g cornflour, sifted

SUITABLE FOR VEGETARIANS

I couldn't write biscuit recipes without including Melting Moments. When I was little, these were one of my first baking ventures. They are so simple but kids love them – baking and eating! They do literally melt in the mouth but don't over cook.

• Beat the butter and icing sugar together. Add the vanilla essence and combine.
• Fold in the sifted flour and cornflour.
• Place baking parchment on your baking tray. Using a teaspoon, place dollops of the mixture evenly over the tray.
• Preheat the halogen oven using the preheat setting or set the temperature to 180°C.
• Bake on the low rack for 10–12 minutes until golden and just firm but not hard.
• Remove from the oven and leave on the tray for a couple of minutes before placing on a cooling rack.
• Store in an airtight container.

Viennese Whirls

MAKES 18–22 DEPENDING ON SIZE

When I was a teenager, my mum and I used to catch a bus to Exeter to go shopping for clothes and generally spend a girlie day together. We would always buy a pack of M&S Viennese Whirls and devour all of them on the journey home. Not much has changed since then – I can still demolish a whole portion of these delicious biscuits! This is a recipe where you really do need to use good quality butter as margarine does not give the same taste or result. Remember that as with most biscuits they will be slightly soft when cooked and will harden once cool.

200g butter
50g icing sugar
½ teaspoon vanilla paste
150g plain flour, sifted
50g cornflour, sifted

SUITABLE FOR VEGETARIANS

- Preheat the halogen oven using the preheat setting or set the temperature to 200°C.
- Beat the butter, icing sugar and vanilla paste together until light and fluffy.
- Gradually add the sifted flour and cornflour until you have a firm but squeezable paste.
- Pop this into your piping bag to create lovely swirly biscuits or, if you don't want to mess around with piping bags, you can carefully spoon dollops onto a greased baking tray, making sure this fits well in your halogen oven. You will probably have enough to do two batches.
- Place on the low rack. (If you have an extension ring, you could bake both batches at the same time but watch the top layer as they will cook faster than the bottom layer.)
- Bake for 10–15 minutes until golden.
- Place on a cooling rack before enjoying. Store in an airtight container once cooled.

Rhubarb Flapjack Bars

400g rhubarb
2 tablespoons sugar
300g butter
3 tablespoons golden
  syrup
200g brown sugar
400g oats
150g flour
1–2 teaspoons
  cinnamon
50g nuts, chopped

SUITABLE FOR VEGETARIANS

These are seriously yummy and quite filling so don't cut them into large slices!

- Preheat the halogen oven using the preheat setting or set the temperature to 190°C.
- Chop the rhubarb into chunks and place in an ovenproof dish. Add the sugar and 1 tablespoon water. Place on the low rack and cook for 10 minutes.
- Meanwhile, place the butter and syrup in an ovenproof dish to melt – you can pop this in the halogen to melt but don't allow it to burn. Stir until combined.
- In a bowl, add the remaining dry ingredients. When the butter/syrup mixture has melted, pour it over the dried mixture and combine.
- Press half the mixture into a greased or lined baking tray, pressing down firmly. Remove the rhubarb from the oven. Stir and spread this over the oat base.
- Add the remaining oat mixture to form a top and press down well.
- Place in the halogen on the low rack and cook for 20–30 minutes until golden.
- Leave to cool before removing from the tin and cutting into slices.

Coconut and Fruit Flapjack

Perfect for packed lunches or picnics. These keep wonderfully in airtight containers until needed. They make a great mid afternoon energy boost if you need it!

- In an ovenproof bowl, add the butter and syrup. Place on the low rack and turn the halogen oven on to 230°C and allow to melt, but not burn! Stir to help the melting process. This should only take a couple of minutes.
- Remove the bowl and add all the remaining ingredients. Stir well.
- Grease a baking tray. Pour on the flapjack mixture and press down firmly.
- Place back in the halogen on the low rack and cook at 180°C for 10–15 minutes.
- Allow to cool before removing from the tin and slicing.
- For added loveliness, coat or dip the slices in dark chocolate.

175g butter (vegans should use dairy-free margarine)
25g golden syrup
125g brown sugar
250g oats
50g desiccated coconut
50g raisins

SUITABLE FOR VEGETARIANS AND VEGANS

Chocolate and Date Fingers

60g plain cooking chocolate (vegans should use dairy-free chocolate)
185g butter (vegans should use dairy-free margarine)
60g brown sugar
1 tablespoon golden syrup
125g dates, roughly chopped
300g oats

SUITABLE FOR VEGETARIANS AND VEGANS

Flapjacks are often seen to be a healthy snack but not really that sexy or yummy. Well, this recipe will hopefully dispel the myth! This is a lovely chocolatey flapjack-style snack and it is very addictive. All you need is a lovely cup of tea, a good book and a comfy sofa – life cannot get any better!

NB: If for some bizarre reason you have some of these left over and need to use them up (I never have!), you could crumble them to use as a delicious topping for a crumble-type pudding or layer in a glass with some stewed apple and crème fraîche, and a grating of dark chocolate and a few chopped hazelnuts to finish – wonderful!

- Preheat the halogen oven using the preheat setting or set the temperature to 180°C.
- In a saucepan, melt the chocolate, butter, sugar and syrup on a low/medium heat. I use a heavy based saucepan and a wooden spoon. Make sure it does not burn so avoid getting distracted and stay with the pan stirring continuously. Once melted, turn the heat off.
- Add the chopped dates and the oats. Mix well until it is thoroughly combined.
- Pour into a greased tin or ovenproof dish. Press down gently with a wooden spoon.
- Place on the low rack and cook for 18–20 minutes until firm and golden. Don't be tempted to overcook as it will result in quite a hard flapjack when you are aiming for a nice soft, chocolatey, yummy oaty slice.
- Leave in the tin to cool. Once cooled, cut into fingers.
- If you are really a chocoholic, you could drizzle with dark chocolate but, to be honest, I can't wait that long and usually devour at least one before they cool.

Raisin Biscuits

Simple dunkable biscuits, which look lovely decorated with a swirl or two of white icing.

- Preheat the halogen oven using the preheat setting or set the temperature to 200°C.
- Beat the butter and sugar together until light and fluffy. Add the egg yolk, vanilla paste and lemon zest and combine well.
- Sift in the flour and mixed spice before adding the raisins. Combine well to form a soft dough.
- At this stage I normally place the dough, wrapped in cling film or a freezer bag, in the fridge for 10 minutes, but you can move on to the next step if you are in a hurry.
- Roll out the dough on a lightly floured board. Aim for 5–8mm thickness. Cut with a biscuit cutter into rounds – you should make 12–15 biscuits.
- Place the biscuits on a greased browning tray. (You can do this in batches or retain the remaining dough to use within a couple of days if stored in the fridge.) Bake on the low rack for 10–15 minutes until golden and just firm but not hard.
- Remove from the oven and leave on the tray for a couple of minutes before placing on a cooling rack.
- Decorate with swirls of white icing. Store in an airtight container.

MAKES 12–15 DEPENDING ON SIZE

110g butter
80g caster sugar
1 egg yolk
½ teaspoon vanilla paste
Zest of 1 lemon
200g plain flour
1 teaspoon mixed spice
50g raisins

SUITABLE FOR VEGETARIANS

Chocolate Concrete

250g plain flour, sifted
75g cocoa, sifted
225g caster sugar
125g butter

SUITABLE FOR VEGETARIANS

My mum used to be the local primary school cook, back in the days when they actually cooked everything fresh on the day rather than the wheeled-in reheating stuff they do in so many schools now. She has lent me her old recipe book from the school cook days and it is fascinating reading – though I have had to break down the quantities somewhat, unless you want to make 150 biscuits! I remember these were served with custard – a bit like a chocolate shortbread according to my mum.

- Preheat the halogen oven using the preheat setting or set the temperature to 175°C.
- In a bowl add the dry ingredients.
- Melt the butter and add this to the dry mix to form a breadcrumb mix.
- Grease a tin thoroughly before pressing in the breadcrumb mixture. As you press with the back of a spoon it will start to smooth out and have a little shine to it.
- Place the tray on the low rack and cook for 20–25 minutes.
- Leave to cool in the tray for a couple of minutes before transferring to the cooling rack. Slice while still warm as it is easier. Serve with custard or on its own.

Date and Walnut Slice

This is a really nice and healthy alternative to a cake. For added indulgence you could add a handful of plain chocolate chips to the mixture.

- Heat the butter in a saucepan over a low/medium heat or in a bowl in the halogen oven, making sure it doesn't burn. Once melted, remove from the heat and stir in the oats, brown sugar and plain flour.
- Press into a lined baking tray to form the base of the slices. I normally line and leave an overhang of baking parchment as I find it easier when it comes to lifting out the cake once cooked. Alternatively, you could use a spring-based baking tray but make sure it is well greased or lined.
- Preheat the halogen oven using the preheat setting or set the temperature to 180°C.
- Beat the sugar and egg together using a food mixer. Once light and fluffy, add the yoghurt and vanilla essence and combine again.
- Add the self-raising flour, dates and most of the walnuts, retaining a few to use on the top of the slices. Once combined, pour this on top of the base. Spread using a spatula to cover the base and sprinkle with the remaining walnuts and a little brown sugar.
- Place on the low rack and cook for 20 minutes until golden and firm to touch.
- Remove from the oven and leave in the tin for 5–10 minutes before slicing.

50g butter
75g oats
30g brown sugar
30g plain flour
75g sugar
1 egg, beaten
2 tablespoons natural yoghurt
1 teaspoon vanilla essence
50g self-raising flour
100g dates, chopped
50g walnuts, chopped

SUITABLE FOR VEGETARIANS

Apple and Almond Slice

2 eggs
250g sour cream
½ teaspoon almond
  essence
120g plain flour, sifted
2 teaspoons baking
  powder, sifted
150g sugar
100g ground almonds
2–3 cooking apples
40g almond slivers

SUITABLE FOR VEGETARIANS

Traditionally this would have been made in a rectangular tray but due to the size constraints of the halogen, you will have to adapt to a round tin or a smaller rectangular tray – you may need two trays depending on the size you opt for. This is the perfect afternoon tea slice: apple, almonds and sweetness – yummy!

• Beat the eggs before adding the sour cream and almond essence.
• Add the sifted flour, baking powder and sugar and combine well before adding the ground almonds.
• Spread half of this mixture over the base of your greased baking tray(s). Top with thinly cut slices of apple before adding the remaining mixture.
• Top with almond slivers.
• Preheat the halogen oven using the preheat setting or set the temperature to 180°C.
• Place the tray on the low rack and bake for 30–40 minutes until the top is golden and firm to touch and a skewer comes out clean when inserted.
• Remove from the oven and leave to cool before slicing. Can be served warm or cold.

Golden Oaties

These are delicious with a cup of tea – very dunkable!

- Place all the dry ingredients in a bowl and combine well. Rub in the butter to form breadcrumbs.
- In a jug mix the milk and golden syrup together. Whisk thoroughly to combine before adding to the dry mixture. Combine well to form a pliable but firm dough.
- Place this in a freezer bag or wrap in cling film and place in the fridge for at least 30 minutes.
- Roll out the dough on a floured surface to about 5mm thick. Using a biscuit or pastry cutter, cut into biscuit rounds and place on a greased browning tray.
- Preheat the halogen oven using the preheat setting or set the temperature to 190°C.
- Place the biscuits on the low rack and cook for 15 minutes until golden. Once cooked, remove from the oven but leave to cool for a minute or two on the baking tray before transferring to the cooling rack.
- Store in an airtight container.

MAKES APPROXIMATELY 10

250g self-raising flour
50g porridge oats
½–1 teaspoon ground
  ginger (optional)
75g golden caster
  sugar
120g butter
1 tablespoon milk
1 tablespoon golden
  syrup

SUITABLE FOR VEGETARIANS

MAKES APPROXIMATELY 10

175g butter

275g brown or golden
sugar

1 egg, beaten

60ml water

1 teaspoon vanilla
extract

140g plain flour, sifted

1 teaspoon
bicarbonate of soda

2–3 teaspoons ground
ginger

350g oats

30g candied ginger,
very finely chopped
(optional)

SUITABLE FOR VEGETARIANS

Ginger Oaties

I love ginger biscuits and these oaties combine the
deliciousness of oats with ginger to create a filling biscuit
perfect for a mid afternoon snack.

- Cream the butter and sugar together using a food
  mixer, until light and fluffy.
- Beat in the egg, water and vanilla before adding the
  sifted dried ingredients and oats. Combine well.
- Add the candied ginger if using, ensuring it is evenly
  distributed.
- Place 1 heaped teaspoon of mixture onto a greased
  or lined browning tray and continue to add to the
  tray, spacing evenly to ensure there is enough room
  for expansion. This mixture should make
  approximately 10 biscuits, so you can bake in two
  batches.
- Preheat the halogen oven using the preheat setting or
  set the temperature to 200°C.
- Place the tray on the low rack and bake for 12
  minutes. Remove and leave the biscuits on the tray
  for 2–3 minutes before transferring to the cooling
  rack.
- Store in an airtight container.

Chocolate Chip Cookies

MAKES 8–10 DEPENDING ON SIZE

My son loves chocolate chip cookies – well, anything with chocolate in it really! At 6 years old he has already perfected this recipe. Make sure you remove these cookies from the halogen when they are still slightly soft but golden to avoid them turning into tough biscuits.

When I first experimented with this recipe, I cooked a batch at 180°C for 15 minutes. Although they cooled okay, they were still a bit soggy and the middles stuck to the tray. Changing to 205°C for 12 minutes improved things. Again they were quite soft when cooked but, once cooled, they were fine. The third batch was baked at 205°C for 15 minutes. These were firmer when removed from the oven and golden brown, but a bit tougher once cooled. The general consensus from my sons is they all taste okay, but the second batch was their favourite.

- Preheat the halogen oven using the preheat setting or set the temperature to 200/205°C.
- In a mixing bowl, combine the butter and sugar until golden. Add the egg and vanilla extract and then the sifted flour and chocolate chips. Combine well.
- On a well greased or lined baking tray, place golfball-sized dollops of the mixture, leaving room for expansion.
- Place on the low rack. You may need to cook in two batches or you could use an extension ring, increasing the height of the oven and enabling you to place trays on two racks (though keep an eye on the top rack as they will cook much faster than the lower rack).
- Cook for 12–15 minutes until golden but still soft (they will harden when cooled). Remove from the oven and place on a cooling rack.
- Store in an airtight container once cooled.

125g butter
125g golden sugar
1 egg
1 teaspoon vanilla extract
175g self-raising flour, sifted
125g plain chocolate chips

SUITABLE FOR VEGETARIANS

MAKES 8–12 DEPENDING ON SIZE

175g butter
150g sugar
1 egg, beaten
1 teaspoon vanilla
  extract
250g flour, sifted
150g white chocolate
  chips or chunks
125g raspberries

SUITABLE FOR VEGETARIANS

Raspberry and White Chocolate Cookies

My favourite combination – delightful and definitely a bit naughty!

- In a mixing bowl, combine the butter and sugar until golden. I normally use my food mixer for this, but you can do it by hand if you prefer. Add the egg and vanilla extract and combine well before adding the sifted flour and white chocolate chips. Once again, combine well.
- Add the raspberries and lightly combine as over stirring will break up the raspberries and result in a soggy mess.
- Preheat the halogen oven using the preheat setting or set the temperature to 190°C.
- On a well greased or lined baking tray, place golfball-sized dollops of the mixture, leaving room for expansion.
- Place on the low rack. You may need to cook in two batches or you could use an extension ring, increasing the height of the oven and enabling you to place trays on two racks (though keep an eye on the top rack as these will cook much faster than the lower rack).
- Cook for 15–20 minutes until golden but still soft (they will harden when cooled). Remove from the oven and leave to cool for at least 5 minutes before placing on a cooling rack. Sometimes, if your raspberries are quite wet, you may need to cook for a little longer as the dough may be wetter than normal.
- Store, if you can avoid the temptation of eating them immediately, in an airtight container once cooled.

Coconut Macaroons

I adore coconut macaroons, especially when drizzled with a little dark chocolate. When we were children, my mum would make them on rice paper – we never tired of eating 'paper'. Just thinking about this makes me want to rush out and buy some rice paper just to see the look of fascination on my younger son's face. So go on, let your inner child escape and invest in some rice paper instead of baking parchment!

- In a clean bowl, beat the egg whites until you get to that frothy stage. Add the cream of tartar and continue to beat until you form soft peaks.
- Add the sugar, a little at a time and follow this by carefully adding the remaining ingredients (apart from the chocolate and rice paper obviously!).
- If you are using rice paper, carefully cut out circles just a little larger than the size of the macaroons when cooked – you can trim them afterwards so don't panic. Place a dollop of the mixture in the centre of the rice paper. If you are not using rice paper, simply place a rounded dollop of the mixture onto greased baking parchment leaving room for expansion.
- Preheat the halogen oven to 160°C. Once the temperature is reached add the macaroons to the low rack and cook for 18–22 minutes until golden on top.
- When cooked, leave to cool on a cooling rack.
- Melt the chocolate in a bowl over a saucepan of hot water making sure the bowl does not touch the water or the chocolate may go thick and lumpy. Then drizzle a little chocolate over the macaroons.
- Store in an airtight container – if they last that long!

MAKES 8–12 DEPENDING ON SIZE

3 large egg whites
¼ teaspoon cream of tartar
100g sugar (caster is best)
250g shredded coconut (not desiccated)
30g ground almonds
1 teaspoon vanilla extract
Rice paper (optional)
30–50g plain or dark chocolate

SUITABLE FOR VEGETARIANS

MAKES 6–8 DEPENDING ON SIZE

110g self-raising flour
30g caster sugar
30g butter
75ml milk

SUITABLE FOR VEGETARIANS

Shortcake

I used to make shortcake as a child. Don't overcook it or you will end up with a hard biscuit/cake – it needs to be soft and crumbly. Serve this with whipped cream and fresh strawberries for a yummy treat or, for a less calorific choice, dunk in a cup of tea!

- Sift the flour into a bowl and add the sugar. Combine well before rubbing in the butter until it looks like breadcrumbs (just like making pastry).
- Add the milk, a little at a time until you have a soft but not wet dough.
- On a floured surface, roll out until it is about 4–5mm thick. You can make this one round plate size and mark out the slices and decorate with a fork, or you can cut with biscuit cutters creating lots of little biscuits.
- Preheat the halogen oven using the preheat setting or set the temperature to 210°C.
- Place the shortcake on a greased browning tray. Cook for 10–12 minutes until golden.
- Turn onto a cooling rack before serving. Once cool, store in an airtight container until needed.

Coconut Shortcake

Another gem from my mum's school cook days. Don't let that put you off as this is a really lovely treat – delicious with a cup of tea! Be careful not to overcook or it will be quite tough.

- Cream the butter and sugar together until fluffy.
- Add the flour and coconut and combine into a dough.
- Roll or press into a greased or lined cake tin or tray. Press down and prick with a fork.
- Place the tray on the low rack and turn the temperature to 180°C (no need to preheat).
- Cook for 30 minutes.
- Cool in the tin. Dust with caster sugar before slicing.

MAKES 8–12 DEPENDING ON SIZE

110g butter
50g sugar
175g self-raising flour
50g desiccated coconut
Caster sugar to dust

SUITABLE FOR VEGETARIANS

MAKES APPROXIMATELY 12

90g butter
60g dark brown sugar
1 egg
60g black treacle
200g plain flour, sifted
½ teaspoon
   bicarbonate of soda
1–2 teaspoons ground
   ginger, depending
   on taste
1 teaspoon cinnamon
Fresh grated nutmeg
   to taste

SUITABLE FOR VEGETARIANS

Gingerbread Men

You can't really do a chapter on biscuits without including gingerbread men! These are ideal for children to decorate and are also perfect for Christmas decorations as they last quite a long time. This is a very simple recipe which makes about 12 gingerbread men, depending on their size. Simply double up the recipe if you want to make more.

• Cream the butter and sugar together until light and fluffy. Add the egg and the treacle and combine well.
• Combine the sifted flour, bicarbonate of soda, ginger and cinnamon and add to the mixture until it forms a pliable but soft dough.
• You can leave the dough in the fridge to settle for at least 30 minutes or for as long as a day if you prefer.
• Roll out onto a floured surface until it reaches a thickness of about 4–5mm and cut into your chosen shapes using biscuit cutters.
• Preheat the halogen oven using the preheat setting or set the temperature to 180°C.
• Place the biscuits onto a greased browning tray. Place on the low rack and cook for 10–15 minutes until they are golden. Leave to cool on the tray for 5 minutes before transferring to a cooling rack.
• Decorate once cool. Store in an airtight container.

Dark Chocolate and Hazelnut Cookies

These are gorgeous. They don't last long enough in our house but, if you are more restrained then we are, why not store them in a lovely vintage glass biscuit jar. They are also perfect as gifts for friends. Simply place them in a cellophane bag and tie with some gingham ribbon.

- Cream the butter and sugar together until light and fluffy. Add the egg and vanilla extract and combine again.
- Mix in the flour and once combined add the chocolate chips and hazelnuts until you have a pliable dough.
- Roll into a sausage and then wrap in cling film or place in a freezer bag and pop in the fridge for an hour.
- When ready, preheat the halogen oven using the preheat setting or set the temperature to 200°C.
- Slice the dough to about a 20mm thickness and place on a greased browning tray.
- Place on the low rack and cook for 12–15 minutes. Don't overcook or they will be too hard.
- Allow to cool on the tray for a couple of minutes before transferring to a cooling rack. Store in an airtight jar until needed.

MAKES 8–12 DEPENDING ON SIZE

125g butter
125g sugar
1 egg
1 teaspoon vanilla extract
200g self-raising flour
50g dark chocolate chips
50g hazelnuts, chopped

SUITABLE FOR VEGETARIANS

MAKES 8–12 DEPENDING ON SIZE

110g butter
1½ tablespoons golden
  syrup
110g oats
110g desiccated
  coconut
110g self-raising flour
110g sugar

SUITABLE FOR VEGETARIANS

Coconut Melts

These are really simple to make – perfect for children. They bake in about 10–12 minutes, as you want them golden but not hard. For an added treat, why not decorate them with a drizzle of dark chocolate.

- Melt the butter and golden syrup until combined.
- Meanwhile, place the dry ingredients in a bowl and mix thoroughly.
- Once combined, pour on the butter mixture and combine again.
- On a greased baking sheet, place 1 teaspoon dollops of the mixture, spread evenly around the tray.
- Preheat the halogen oven using the preheat setting or set the temperature to 170°C.
- Place on the low rack and cook for 10–12 minutes until golden. Don't overcook or they will be too hard.
- Cool for a couple of minutes before transferring to the cooling rack. Store in an airtight jar until needed.

Spicy Christmas Biscuits

These are perfect for Christmas but, really, why wait? They are lovely, dunkable biscuits with a nice cuppa.

- Beat the butter, sugar and syrup together until light and fluffy. Add the flour, cinnamon, ginger and mixed spice and combine well.
- Stir in the semolina until you have formed a dough. Roll into a sausage shape, wrap in cling film and pop in the fridge for half an hour.
- On a floured surface, cut 4mm-thick slices from your sausage shape – flatten slightly before placing on a greased baking tray.
- Preheat the halogen oven using the preheat setting or set the temperature to 200°C.
- Bake on the low rack for 10–15 minutes until golden and just firm but not hard.
- Remove from the oven and leave on the tray for a couple of minutes before placing on a cooling rack.
- Decorate with swirls of white icing. Store in an airtight container.

MAKES 8–12 DEPENDING ON SIZE

110g butter
110g sugar
4 tablespoons golden syrup
200g self-raising flour
1 teaspoon cinnamon
1 teaspoon ground ginger
1 teaspoon mixed spice
110g semolina

SUITABLE FOR VEGETARIANS

Tart It Up and Roll It Out

'The queen of hearts, she made some tarts, all on a summer's day, the knave of hearts, he stole the tarts and took them clean away' – The Hive Collection of Scraps, 1782

If you can master the art of pastry making, your world of cooking will open up immensely. There are so many great pastry recipes and, for those who don't want to get their hands dirty, even readymade pastry to choose from. Readymade puff pastry and filo pastry are great to have as a standby – many lovely dishes can be made with the minimum of effort.

There are some basic rules to good pastry making, but mainly it is child's play. Shortcrust pastry is basically half fat to flour and you can combine with water, egg or even juice (I use orange juice quite a lot for sweet pastries). If you are making your own pastry, avoid handling it too much. A food processor is a great way to produce pastry without mess or unnecessary handling. Pastry likes to be cool. (If you have ever let a child play with pastry you will have seen that after some minutes of playing, the pastry goes a yucky shade of grey and starts to get a bit soft and soggy.) I have found that placing the pastry in the fridge for 10 minutes before rolling out produces the best results. Nigella (whom I am in awe of) recommends placing the flour and fat, once roughly coated in flour, in the freezer for 10 minutes before moving on to the next step. Delia recommends using frozen butter, grated into the flour to make the perfect but easy flaky pastry.

For sweet pastry I use icing sugar or superfine caster sugar and an egg yolk. I then combine with water or orange juice. I may add seeds, herbs or spices if I want to give it a lift. For savoury pastry, I prefer to use a wholegrain or multigrain/granary flour as I love the texture and taste of the seeds and whole wheat. I don't make my own puff pastry as readymade or frozen is so easily available and easy to use. I remember making puff pastry when I did home economics O Level at school and the endless folding and adding butter seemed to go on forever. I prefer to reserve this type of energy for bread making!

When rolling out your pastry, always use a floured surface. Rachel Allen uses cling film and rolls the pastry directly onto this as she finds it is easier when lifting off pastry and also avoids mess. I sometimes use some baking parchment if I am in a hurry and don't want to do masses of clearing up afterwards, but generally baking time for me inevitably means floured surfaces. Give your rolling pin a rub with a little flour to avoid the pastry sticking. Flour both sides of the pastry. If you are lining a round dish, start with a circular piece of pastry. Flour both sides of the pastry and roll straight in front of you, turn 90°, roll again, turn, roll and continue until you have reached the desired size. You can turn the pastry over during this process if you prefer, but remember to keep both sides lightly dusted with flour.

When you are ready to pick the pastry up and transfer to your pastry dish, hook one side of the pastry over the rolling pin, then roll the pin so the rest of the pastry lifts up and ends up draped over the rolling pin, then simply roll onto the dish. Once pressed down, use a knife to trim the edges.

The halogen is a great machine but a word of warning for those who love pastry: I have found that the bottoms of tarts or pies can sometimes get a soggy or even a bit raw if you are not careful. For this reason, I prefer to blind bake any pastry bases before adding my fillings. With puff or filo pastry I always use the browning tray as this helps cook the base. If I am making larger dishes, I sometimes use my pizza tray which has holes in it allowing the base to cook. If you are making sausage rolls or pasties, you may find that turning them over for the last 5–10 minutes of cooking helps the bottoms brown and crisp to your desired taste. If you are concerned, why not just add a pastry top to your pie? Chicken pie is fantastic with a puff pastry top, especially when sprinkled with sesame seeds and black pepper.

Apple and Blackberry Frangipane Tart

150g plain flour
75g butter
75g sugar
1 egg, beaten
1 tablespoon water
125g butter
125g sugar
2 eggs
125g ground almonds
1 tablespoon plain
  flour
1–2 teaspoons
  cinnamon
2 apples, sliced
40g blackberries
2 tablespoons apricot
  jam

SUITABLE FOR VEGETARIANS

I love the look of this tart almost as much as the taste. Sprinkle with icing sugar before serving. Delicious hot or cold.

- To make your pastry, place 150g of plain flour in a bowl. Add 75g of butter and rub to form a texture similar to breadcrumbs. Add 75g of sugar and combine well.
- Add 1 beaten egg and 1 tablespoon of water and combine to form a dough. Then place the dough in the fridge to rest while you continue with the rest of the recipe.
- Preheat the halogen oven using the preheat setting or set the temperature to 200°C.
- Roll out the pastry and line a greased flan dish (make sure this fits in your halogen oven). Prick with a fork and place on the low rack for 10–15 minutes (baking blind). You can use baking beans over a sheet of baking parchment if you want to prevent air bubbles in the pastry.
- Whilst that is cooking, beat 125g of butter and 125g of sugar together until light and fluffy. Gradually add 2 eggs. When this is well beaten, add the ground almonds, 1 tablespoon of flour and cinnamon. Beat well.
- Pour this onto the pastry case. Over the top, place the apple slices in a nice even pattern, around the dish. Add the blackberries in between the apple slices and press into the sponge mixture.

- Turn the temperature down to 180°C. Return the flan dish to the low rack and bake for 30 minutes until the apples are cooked and the sponge has risen – test the sponge to make sure it is cooked; if not, return for another 5–10 minutes. Remove from the oven immediately once cooked or your pastry will become soggy.
- Gently heat the apricot jam, stirring continuously to avoid burning. Once it is runny, brush over the baked apples to form a glaze, ensuring the top is well covered. Return to the halogen for 5 more minutes.
- Serve hot or cold with ice-cream, crème fraîche or just on its own.

Apple Turnovers

½ pack puff pastry
Stewed apple or 2
   cooking apples,
   finely sliced
Sugar and cinnamon
   to taste (optional)
Beaten egg or milk
Brown sugar to
   sprinkle

SUITABLE FOR VEGETARIANS

These are great if you have any spare puff pastry or stewed apple to use up. Stewed apple is easiest, but you can simply slice some cooking apples into the centre of the pastry, add some sugar and off you go.

- Preheat the halogen oven using the preheat setting or turn the temperature to 200°C.
- Roll out the puff pastry to about 4–5mm thick. Cut into squares of approximately 15–20cm.
- Place 2–3 teaspoons of stewed apple or apple slices in the centre of each puff pastry square. If you are using apple slices, add a sprinkle of sugar and cinnamon to taste.
- Using a pastry brush, brush the egg or milk around the edges of the square. I normally fold diagonally to form a triangle. Secure the edges by crimping.
- Coat with milk or egg and sprinkle with brown sugar.
- Place on the low rack and bake for 15–18 minutes until golden. If the bottoms are not done to your satisfaction, carefully turn them over and cook for another 5 minutes.
- Place on a cooling rack or serve warm with a dollop of cream or crème fraîche.

Simple Cheating Eccles Cakes

These were my dad's favourite when I was growing up. Funny, I never really liked them when I was a child – a bit like garibaldi biscuits ... we thought they were packed with dead flies! I have matured since then and found I really love them. They don't last long in our home, so here is a very fast and easy recipe to suit the craving.

½ pack puff pastry
½ small jar of
   mincemeat
25g melted butter
Sprinkling of brown
   sugar

SUITABLE FOR VEGETARIANS

- Preheat the halogen oven using the preheat setting or turn the temperature to 200°C.
- Roll out the puff pastry to about 4–5mm thick. Cut into squares of approximately 15–20cm.
- Place 2–3 teaspoons of mincemeat in the centre of each puff pastry square.
- Using a pastry brush, brush the melted butter around the edges of each square. I normally fold diagonally, bringing each corner to the centre to form an envelope/parcel. Alternatively, you can simply fold over and secure either to form a rectangle or a triangle.
- On a floured surface, turn the cakes over so that the seam is on the bottom. Apply a bit of pressure on your rolling pin or fingers and gently roll the cakes flat, being careful not to split the pastry.
- Using a sharp knife, score 2–3 slits in the top of the cakes. Brush with butter and a sprinkle of brown sugar before placing on a greased browning tray.
- Place on the low rack and bake for 15–18 minutes until golden. If the base of the cakes are not done to your satisfaction, carefully turn them over and cook for another 5 minutes until golden top and bottom.
- Place on a cooling rack before serving.

150g plain flour
75g butter
75g sugar
1 egg, beaten
1 tablespoon water
1kg cooking apples
Lemon juice
15g butter
60g sugar
1–2 teaspoons
   cinnamon
1 tablespoon semolina
3 tablespoons apricot
   jam

SUITABLE FOR VEGETARIANS

French Apple Tart

This is a lovely dish. The recipe includes instructions for making the pastry case but, if you aren't up to making your own, you could buy readymade sweet pastry or ready-cooked pastry cases, but these will obviously be more expensive than making your own.

- To make your pastry, place the flour in a bowl. Add 75g of butter and rub to form a texture similar to breadcrumbs. Add 75g of sugar and combine well.
- Add the beaten egg and 1 tablespoon of water and combine to form a dough. Then place the dough in the fridge to rest while you continue with the rest of the recipe.
- Peel and thinly slice the apples and place them in water with a little lemon juice.
- Preheat the halogen oven using the preheat setting or set the temperature to 200°C.
- Roll out the pastry and line a greased flan dish (make sure this fits in your halogen oven). Prick with a fork and place on the low rack for 15 minutes (baking blind). You can use baking beans over a sheet of baking parchment if you want to prevent air bubbles in the pastry.
- Whilst that is cooking, remove a third of the apple slices and place them in a pan to soften with a little butter, a drizzle of water and 1 dessertspoon of sugar. Stir until soft before adding almost all the cinnamon.

- Remove the pastry case and sprinkle over 1 tablespoon of semolina (this helps prevent a soggy pastry bottom) and smooth on the pureed apple. Over the top of this, place the apple slices in a nice even pattern, fanning out and overlapping slightly around the flan dish. Sprinkle with sugar and the remaining cinnamon.
- Return to the low rack and bake for 25–30 minutes until the apples are cooked. Remove from the oven immediately once cooked to avoid the pastry going soggy with the condensation of the oven.
- Gently heat the apricot jam, stirring continuously to avoid burning. Once it is runny, brush over the baked apples ensuring the top is well covered.
- Serve hot or cold with ice-cream, crème fraîche or just on its own.

Jam Turnovers

½ pack puff pastry
Jam of your choice
Beaten egg or milk
25g melted butter
Sprinkling of brown
   sugar

SUITABLE FOR VEGETARIANS

If I am making some Eccles Cakes, my younger son usually demands to help and inevitably wants to make Jam Turnovers. The recipe is similar to Eccles Cakes, so I would suggest combining both to save time and money!

- Preheat the halogen oven using the preheat setting or turn the temperature to 200°C.
- Roll out the puff pastry to about 4–5mm thick. Cut into squares of approximately 15–20cm.
- Place 2–3 teaspoons of jam in the centre of each puff pastry square.
- Using a pastry brush, brush the egg or milk around the edges of the square. I normally fold diagonally to form a triangle. Secure the edges by crimping.
- Brush with butter and a sprinkle of brown sugar before placing on a greased browning tray.
- Place on the low rack and bake for 15–18 minutes until golden. If the base of the cakes are not done to your satisfaction, carefully turn them over and cook for another 5 minutes until golden top and bottom.
- Place on a cooling rack before serving.

Lemon Tart

I love lemon tart and this recipe is so simple anyone can make it. You can cheat and use a pre-baked pastry case or ready-to-roll sweet shortcrust pasty or simply follow the recipe from scratch. This recipe uses 4 egg yolks, so why not use the egg whites to make a meringue for a Pavlova or Eton Mess?

- Place the flour and icing sugar in a bowl and combine well. Rub in the butter to form breadcrumbs. Combine with 1 egg yolk and a little water if necessary until you have a firm dough. Place this dough in the fridge to rest for 5–10 minutes.
- Once rested, line a greased flan tin with your pastry. Prick with a fork and place a sheet of baking parchment over the top. You can add baking beans if you wish to prevent the flan from rising.
- Preheat the halogen oven using the preheat setting or set the temperature to 190°C.
- Place the flan on the low rack and cook for 10–15 minutes.
- While this is cooking you can prepare the filling by mixing the condensed milk, lemon juice and zest and 3 egg yolks together. Mix thoroughly.
- Pour this mixture onto your pastry base and place back in the halogen oven. Cook for another 10–12 minutes.
- Remove and leave to cool. Sprinkle with icing sugar before serving.

100g plain flour
40g icing sugar
50g butter
1 egg yolk
1 400g tin of condensed milk
Juice and zest of 3 lemons
3 egg yolks
Icing sugar to sprinkle

SUITABLE FOR VEGETARIANS

Raspberry, Hazelnut and Dark Chocolate Horns

½ pack puff pastry

Butter

Milk or beaten egg to brush

Brown sugar to sprinkle

200g Greek yoghurt (I use Total 0%)

2 tablespoons low fat crème fraîche

1 teaspoon vanilla paste

50g hazelnuts, finely chopped

150g raspberries, frozen or fresh

100g dark chocolate

SUITABLE FOR VEGETARIANS

My mum used to make cream horns when we were children. They were very exciting but inevitably filled with jam and oozing with cream – so much so we normally ended up with cream oozing down our jumpers when we took a bite. This recipe is a much healthier option but still retains the excitement and impressive presentation. I like the kitsch look they create when served on a glass cake stand. You should be able to pick up the metal moulds needed to make the horns from a cook shop.

- Roll out the puff pastry, quite thin, approximately 2–3cm thick.
- Cut into 1cm strips, long enough to wrap around the cone moulds – roughly 12cm long.
- Butter the metal horns to prevent the pastry from sticking. Carefully wrap the strips of pastry around the cone, starting at the base and making sure you overlap the pastry slightly as you go up the cone. Seal securely. Repeat this for the remaining cones.
- Carefully brush with milk or beaten egg and sprinkle with brown sugar. Place the cones, seal-side down, onto a greased tray or baking sheet.
- Preheat the halogen oven using the preheat setting or set the temperature to 210°C.
- Place on the low rack and cook for 15–20 minutes until golden. Carefully turn the horns so the underside is showing and cook for another 5 minutes to brown off the bottoms.
- Remove immediately and allow to cool.

- Meanwhile, mix the yoghurt and crème fraîche together. Once combined, add the vanilla paste and the hazelnuts.
- In another bowl, place half the raspberries and gently break up with a fork to roughly mash them.
- Once the horns are cool, carefully remove the moulds. Gently twist the metal moulds and they should come loose, but don't force them!
- Place a bowl over a pan of boiling water and melt the chocolate gently. Once melted, dip the open ends of the cones into the chocolate, to create a nice chocolate lip of about 3–4cm. Place on the cooling rack to set.
- Once set, place a spoonful of raspberry mash in the bottom of the horn, followed by the yoghurt mixture.
- Serve on a plate with a drizzle of mashed raspberries and a handful of fresh raspberries.

Raspberry Cream Tartlets

125g plain flour
1 tablespoon caster
  sugar
50g butter
1 egg yolk
2 eggs
150ml sour cream
1 teaspoon vanilla
  essence
200g raspberries

SUITABLE FOR VEGETARIANS

These are yummy hot or cold. When baking pastry in the halogen, always blind bake as it avoids a soggy pastry bottom. You can cheat and buy pre-cooked pastry cases if you are in a hurry.

- In a bowl, combine the plain flour and sugar. Rub in the butter and add the egg yolk. Combine with a little water to form a dough.
- Roll out on a floured board to a 4mm thickness.
- Line the greased tartlet cases and trim. Line with baking parchment and add a few baking beans.
- Preheat the halogen oven using the preheat setting or set the temperature to 180°C.
- Place on the low rack and cook for 10 minutes, remove the beans and parchment and cook for another 5 minutes. Remove from the oven immediately.
- Meanwhile, whisk the eggs and combine with the sour cream and vanilla essence. Line the pastry cases with a scattering of raspberries before pouring on the creamy mixture.
- Place back in the halogen on the low rack and cook for 20–30 minutes until the tartlets are set and golden.
- Serve hot or cold. For added appeal, why not dust with a little icing sugar and serve with a few raspberries and mint leaves.

Treacle Tart

You can't really have a chapter on pies and tarts without including treacle tart. This is a real traditional favourite and was particularly so in my childhood. We often forget how simple yet satisfying this recipe is. I prefer to leave the top open but you could add some decorative lattice swirls or pastry twists.

- To make the pastry, place the flour in a bowl. Add 75g of butter and rub to form a texture similar to breadcrumbs. Add the sugar and combine well.
- Add the beaten egg and 1 tablespoon of water and combine to form a dough. Then place this in the fridge to rest.
- Preheat the halogen oven using the preheat setting or set the temperature to 200°C.
- Roll out the pastry and line a greased flan dish (make sure it fits in your halogen oven). Prick with a fork and place on the low rack for 15 minutes (baking blind). You can use baking beans over a sheet of baking parchment if you want to prevent air bubbles in the pastry.
- Melt 30g of butter and the golden syrup in a saucepan on a low/medium heat.
- Add the breadcrumbs, cornflakes, lemon zest and juice and the ground ginger. Combine well before placing in the pastry case.
- Place back in the halogen on the same heat, on the low rack for another 15–20 minutes.
- Serve hot or cold. Delicious!

150g plain flour
75g butter
75g sugar
1 egg, beaten
1 tablespoon water
30g butter
200g golden syrup
60g breadcrumbs
30g cornflakes, crushed
Zest of 1 lemon
Juice of ½ lemon (use the whole lemon if you prefer a more lemony taste)
½ teaspoon ground ginger

SUITABLE FOR VEGETARIANS

Open Crumbly Apple, Raisin and Cinnamon Pie

100g plain flour
40g icing sugar
50g butter
1 egg yolk
600g cooking apples,
    cored and sliced
½ teaspoon nutmeg
2 teaspoons cinnamon
75g raisins
110g brown sugar
75g oats
50g breadcrumbs
40g nuts, chopped
40g plain flour
75g butter
1–2 tablespoons
    semolina or 1 egg
    white

SUITABLE FOR VEGETARIANS

This is a simple but wonderful pie that never ceases to delight and comfort. Serve with vanilla ice-cream for a perfectly satisfying pud! When baking pastry in the halogen, always blind bake as it avoids a soggy pastry bottom. You can cheat and buy pre-cooked pastry cases if you are in a hurry.

- Place the flour and icing sugar in a bowl and combine well. Rub in the butter to form breadcrumbs. Combine with the egg yolk and a little water if necessary until you have a firm dough. Place this dough in the fridge to rest for 5–10 minutes.
- Once rested, roll out the dough and line a greased flan tin. Prick with a fork and place a sheet of baking parchment over the top. You can add baking beans if you wish to prevent the flan from rising.
- Preheat the halogen oven using the preheat setting or set the temperature to 190°C.
- Place the flan tin on the low rack and cook for 10–15 minutes.
- While this is cooking, prepare the filling by placing the apple in a saucepan with a tablespoon or two of water (not too much as you don't want the apple to be too wet). Add the nutmeg, cinnamon, raisins and sugar and cook until the apple starts to soften, but don't let it become mushy.
- While the apple and pastry are cooking, combine the oats, breadcrumbs, nuts, flour and butter in a bowl. If you have an extra sweet tooth you could add a spoonful or two of brown sugar or even some dark chocolate chips. Leave to one side until later.

- Some people wash the baked pastry case with egg white as it is supposed to almost waterproof the pastry – I will leave this up to you. Personally, I sprinkle with a spoonful or two of semolina as I find this does a similar thing.
- Place the apple in the prepared pastry case. Sprinkle the crumble mixture over the top.
- Place back in the halogen on the low rack at the same temperature. Cook for another 15–20 minutes until golden.
- Serve with vanilla ice-cream.

Easy Chocolate Flan

100g plain flour
40g icing sugar
50g butter
1 egg yolk
30g cocoa
30g cornflour
425ml full fat milk
30g sugar
½ teaspoon vanilla
  extract
50g dark chocolate,
  grated

SUITABLE FOR VEGETARIANS

This was one of the first recipes I made in Home Economics. It is very simple and quite yummy. I used to travel home on the school bus – the drawback on HE day was the inability to resist eating my creations. I seem to remember that by the time I got it home, this chocolate pie had rather a lot of finger marks in it!

The original recipe just combined milk, cocoa, sugar and cornflour, but I prefer to add vanilla extract and a little dark chocolate for an extra kick. I normally grate in a little Willie Harcourt's Pure Cacao as I love the flavour and the fact that it's a healthy chocolate option. I also use a sweet shortcrust pastry, but feel free to use just flour and butter if you prefer. Serve with piped whipped cream for a 1970s retro look.

- Place the flour and icing sugar in a bowl and combine well. Rub in the butter to form breadcrumbs. Combine with the egg yolk and a little water if necessary until you have a firm dough. Place in the fridge to rest for 5–10 minutes.
- Once rested, roll out the dough and line a greased flan tin. Prick with a fork and place a sheet of baking parchment over the top. You can add baking beans if you wish to prevent the flan from rising.
- Preheat the halogen oven using the preheat setting or set the temperature to 190°C.
- Place the flan tin on the low rack and cook for 10–15 minutes.
- Whilst this is cooking, prepare the filling by mixing the cocoa and cornflour together with a little of the milk.

- Place the remaining milk in a saucepan and bring to the boil, in a similar way to making custard. Once heated, add the cocoa mixture, sugar and vanilla extract. If you are using dark chocolate, add this now. Stir continually as it will thicken. I prefer to do this on a low/medium heat to avoid burning the bottom of the pan.
- Once thickened, pour onto the cooked flan case.
- Leave to cool before piping on whipped cream.

Almond Tart

150g plain flour
75g butter
75g sugar
1 egg, beaten
1 tablespoon water
75g butter
75g sugar
75g semolina
1 egg
1–2 teaspoons almond
  essence
1 teaspoon baking
  powder
Raspberry jam
Sliced almonds
  (optional)

SUITABLE FOR VEGETARIANS

This is another recipe from an old scrapbook. It is really a
Bakewell Tart in style. I find it nice and easy and the kids love it
if I cover it with icing. Lovely with a cup of tea.

- To make the pastry, place the flour in a bowl. Add 75g
  of butter and rub to form a texture similar to
  breadcrumbs. Add 75g of sugar and combine well.
- Add the beaten egg and 1 tablespoon of water and
  combine to form a dough. Then place the dough in
  the fridge to rest while you continue with the rest of
  the recipe.
- Preheat the halogen oven using the preheat setting or
  set the temperature to 200°C.
- Roll out the pastry and line a greased flan dish (make
  sure this fits in your halogen). Prick with a fork and
  place on the low rack for 15 minutes (baking blind).
  You can use baking beans over a sheet of baking
  parchment if you want to prevent air bubbles in the
  pastry.
- When the pastry has cooked, melt 75g of butter in a
  saucepan on a low heat. Stir in 75g of sugar and the
  semolina. Stir well before adding the egg, almond
  essence and baking powder.
- Line the pastry with a layer of jam before pouring on
  the almond mixture.
- Decorate with a few almond slices if you wish.
- Bake on the low rack at the same temperature for 20
  minutes until golden.
- Leave to cool before slicing.

French Prune Tart

A lovely grown-up recipe I discovered in the scrapbook belonging to my great aunt Sylvia. Don't be put off by the prunes – they are delicious, plump and sweet. Enjoy!

- Place the prunes and apricots in a bowl with the liqueur and leave to rest for at least 30 minutes.
- Meanwhile you can make the pastry. Sift the flour into a bowl, add the semolina and sugar and combine well.
- Rub in the butter until you form breadcrumbs. Add the beaten eggs to form a dough. Place this in cling film or a freezer bag and chill in the freezer.
- Melt the butter. Pour into a (25cm or 10in) greased flan tin and sprinkle with the brown sugar. Place the fruit onto the butter and sugar.
- Roll or press out the dough until it is large enough to cover the fruit. Place over the fruit and gently press down.
- Preheat the halogen oven using the preheat setting or set the temperature to 190°C.
- Place the tin on the low rack and cook for 25–30 minutes.
- Turn out onto a serving plate so the fruit is face upwards (just like an upside-down cake).
- Serve hot or warm with cream or yoghurt.

250g pitted prunes
110g ready-to-eat dried apricots
3–4 tablespoons Amaretto liqueur
225g plain flour
75g semolina
75g caster sugar
175g butter
2 eggs, beaten
50g butter, melted
75g brown sugar

The Big Finish – Delightful Desserts

'There is no sincerer love than the love of food'
– George Bernard Shaw

Personally, I think the best part of a meal is the pudding. If I am in a restaurant, I would actually prefer to have a delicious starter and a pudding and come away feeling comfortable than squeeze in a pudding (I can never resist) and then suffer the aftermath of overeating. It is foolish to expect me to restrain myself – puddings are meant to be enjoyed and I certainly do that! Here are some simple yet delicious recipes I hope you will enjoy as much as I have. Some of these can be eaten hot or cold so they are ideal for alfresco dining or that picnic in the park.

For more inspiration, look at Chapter 7, Tart It Up and Roll It Out, as it contains many recipes suitable for puddings and desserts.

SERVES 6

115g butter
250g self-raising flour
100g caster sugar
3 egg yolks
2–3 tablespoons water
100g raspberries
3 egg whites
50g sugar
400g cream cheese
1 teaspoon vanilla
  essence or paste
Extra raspberries to
  serve

SUITABLE FOR VEGETARIANS

Baked Raspberry Cheesecake

If you don't want raspberry, you could opt for other berries such as blueberry or even sultanas soaked in liqueur.

- In a bowl cut the butter into small pieces and add the flour, rubbing the butter into it to form fine breadcrumbs.
- Mix together the sugar and egg yolks and 2 tablespoons of water.
- Add to the flour and mix to form a soft dough. If necessary, add another tablespoon of water.
- Spread the mixture into a greased or lined tin with a spring clip, pressing down firmly. (Make sure the tin fits in the halogen oven.) Sprinkle the raspberries on top of the dough.
- Beat the egg whites until stiff. Add the sugar and beat for 1 minute.
- In a bowl beat the cream cheese and vanilla and then fold in the egg whites. Spread the mixture over the raspberries.
- Preheat the halogen oven using the preheat setting or set the temperature to 180°C.
- Place on the low rack and bake for 35–45 minutes until firm and golden.
- Leave to cool and serve with a scattering of fresh raspberries as a garnish.

Raspberry Healthy Brûlée

This was one of the first experiments I made using the halogen oven so I thought I would also include it in this book as it is a good confidence booster. It is a really yummy dessert that takes just minutes to prepare. I always have frozen raspberries in my freezer and yoghurt and crème fraîche in my fridge. This dessert looks and tastes far more impressive than it really is and the good news is that it is actually quite healthy! You can experiment by using blueberries or summer fruits instead of the raspberries.

- If you are using frozen raspberries, place them on your serving dish and place on the high rack in the halogen oven on the thaw setting for 10 minutes.
- Meanwhile, mix the yoghurt and crème fraîche together in a bowl. Once combined, add the vanilla paste and stir well.
- Remove the raspberries from the halogen. I tend to serve this in one serving dish (big enough for 4–6 portions), but you could use individual serving dishes, though make sure they are heatproof. I keep the raspberries in the dish I thawed them in as it is heatproof. If you are using a different dish, or ramekin dishes, place the raspberries at the bottom.
- Spoon over the yoghurt mixture, then a sprinkle of brown sugar – enough to form a generous layer to make the crème brûlée effect.
- Place back in the halogen oven on the high rack. Turn to the highest setting (usually 250°C) for 3–4 minutes, allowing the brown sugar to melt and caramelise. The beauty of the halogen oven is that you are able to see this cooking and avoid burning.
- Serve and enjoy!

SERVES 4–6

200g frozen raspberries (or you can use fresh)
350–400g Greek yoghurt (I use Total 0%)
3 tablespoons low fat crème fraîche
1 teaspoon vanilla paste
3–4 tablespoons brown sugar

SUITABLE FOR VEGETARIANS

SERVES 4–6

90g white bread,
   cubed
45g sugar
420ml milk
1 teaspoon vanilla
   extract or paste
45g butter
2 eggs, separated
60g caster sugar
3 tablespoons jam
   (I use raspberry but
   feel free to use
   whatever you prefer)

SUITABLE FOR VEGETARIANS

Queen of Puddings

My mum used to make this for us when we were children.
Comforting puddings are making a well-earned revival – so
much nicer than shop-bought processed puddings.

• Preheat the halogen oven using the preheat setting or
  turn the temperature to 180°C.
• Grease an ovenproof dish.
• Place the cubed bread in a bowl. Sprinkle with the
  sugar.
• In a saucepan, heat the milk, vanilla and butter to
  almost boiling point and then pour over the bread
  and sugar mixture. When cool, add the egg yolks and
  whisk until smooth.
• Pour this into the greased ovenproof dish. Place on
  the low rack and cook for 30–35 minutes until set.
• While this is cooking, beat the egg whites until they
  form soft peaks, gradually adding half the caster
  sugar. Melt the jam on a low heat as you don't want to
  burn it.
• Spread the jam over the set mixture. Top this with the
  whisked egg whites. Sprinkle with the remaining
  caster sugar.
• Place back in the oven and cook for another 8–10
  minutes until golden.

Baked Bananas with Dark Chocolate Sauce

SERVES 4

This recipe also appeared in my previous halogen cookbook but it was so popular, it has to be added to this chapter. Simple recipes are always the best and this is hard to beat. For an extra twist, why not add some chopped hazelnuts or, for fans of chocolate orange, a teaspoon of orange essence to the chocolate sauce. So simple but it tastes amazing.

- Preheat the halogen oven using the preheat setting or set the temperature to 180°C.
- Place the bananas in an ovenproof tray in their skins and bake on the low rack for 10 minutes, or until the skin goes completely black.
- Meanwhile, melt the chocolate, butter, honey and cocoa in a bowl over a saucepan of water or a bain marie.
- When you are ready to serve, pour the chocolate mixture over the peeled bananas and finish with a generous dollop of crème fraîche or ice-cream.

4 bananas
120g bar of dark
  chocolate
25g butter
1–2 tablespoons honey
1 tablespoon cocoa
A spoonful of crème
  fraîche or ice-cream
  per serving

SUITABLE FOR VEGETARIANS

SERVES 4–6

8 egg whites
300g caster sugar
1 tablespoon cornflour
3 teaspoons vinegar
500ml double cream
350g fresh raspberries
2–3 passion fruit

SUITABLE FOR VEGETARIANS

Raspberry and Passion Fruit Pavlova

I adore pavlova. You can use the fruit I have suggested here, or use your own variations. I saw Nigella use passion fruit in her pavlova and it looked so gorgeous I just had to give it a try – now it has become a family favourite.

- In a clean bowl, whip the egg whites until they form soft peaks. Add the sugar, a little at a time, and continue to beat until the egg whites stiffen.
- Again, I have followed Nigella's recommendation: carefully fold in the cornflour and vinegar. It really does make a much chewier meringue – once converted, you will never change this!
- Place a piece of baking parchment on a browning tray. Leaving a gap of about 10–15mm all around the edge of the tray, place thick dollops of the meringue into the centre to form a thick circle. Smooth where needed, especially the edges.
- Preheat the halogen oven using the preheat setting or set the temperature to 200°C.
- Place the meringue on the low rack and immediately turn down to 135–150°C depending on your machine. (Digital will only let you choose 125°C or 150°C and ideally you need somewhere in the middle, but keep an eye on things and remove earlier.)
- Bake for 1–1½ hours until cooked. Remove and cool. You can place the meringue in an airtight container and store until needed or decorate once cooled.

- I place the meringue onto a nice decorative dish or cake stand before filling – this avoids having to move it once filled.
- Whip the cream and spread this over the meringue base. Decorate with the fruit. I personally like the juice of the raspberries, so I remove about a third of the raspberries and gently crush them. I use the whole raspberries to decorate and then drizzle over with the crushed raspberries.
- Cut the passion fruit in half and scoop out the flesh, pouring this over the raspberries.
- Serve while it is oozing with juice.

SERVES 4–6

8–12 plums
Sugar
2–3 tablespoons water
Cointreau or Amaretto
    liqueur (optional)
1–2 tablespoons honey
Cinnamon
Sliced almonds
Custard, crème fraîche
    or ice-cream to serve

SUITABLE FOR VEGETARIANS
AND VEGANS

Honey Roasted Plums with Almonds

It is not just vegetables that can be roasted: these plums are delicious when slow cooked and they are perfect for the halogen.

- Preheat the halogen oven using the preheat setting or set the temperature to 180°C.
- Wash the plums. While still wet, roll them in sugar and place on a greased or buttered baking tray or ovenproof dish. Add the water or, if you are feeling a bit naughty, some liqueur of your choice.
- Place on the low rack and cook for 10 minutes.
- Drizzle over the honey and sprinkle with some cinnamon and almonds before cooking again for another 10–15 minutes until the plums are cooked.
- Serve with custard, crème fraîche or ice-cream.

Cheat's Ginger and Apple Layer

Such a simple dish using some store-cupboard staples. It can be thrown together in minutes – perfect for a quick and easy dessert.

- Place the chopped apple in a saucepan with the water and sugar. Cook until it starts to soften, but still has a bite (not pureed). Add the sultanas and cinnamon and combine well.
- Preheat the halogen oven using the preheat setting or set the temperature to 180°C.
- Grease an ovenproof dish.
- Crumble a layer of ginger cake in the bottom of the ovenproof dish. Over this, add a layer of apple. Repeat finishing with a ginger cake top.
- Pour over the orange juice and zest. Sprinkle with the coconut and 1 tablespoon of brown sugar.
- Place on the low rack and cook for 15–20 minutes.
- Serve with Homemade Custard or Butterscotch Sauce (see page 187) … delicious!

SERVES 4–6

700g Bramley apples, cored, peeled and diced
2 tablespoons water
50g brown sugar
50g sultanas
1 teaspoon cinnamon
1 small ginger cake, crumbled
Juice and zest of 1 orange
1 tablespoon desiccated coconut
1 tablespoon brown sugar

SUITABLE FOR VEGETARIANS

SERVES 4–6

150–200g strawberries, quartered or thickly sliced
1 tub of cream cheese
1 tub of Greek yoghurt
2–3 tablespoons crème fraîche
1 teaspoon vanilla paste
Juice and zest of 1–2 lemons
6–8 digestive biscuits
2–3 tablespoons brown sugar

SUITABLE FOR VEGETARIANS

Upside Down Strawberry Cheesecake

I am a big fan of cheesecake and this is a yummy variation of the classic recipe.

- Prepare the strawberries and place in the bottom of an ovenproof serving dish – this needs to be big enough for 4–6 servings (or you can use individual ramekin dishes).
- Combine the cream cheese, yoghurt and crème fraîche. Add the vanilla paste and stir well. Roughly peel the lemon with a vegetable peeler to remove the zest. Chop this finely before adding to the cream cheese mixture. Add the juice of 1 lemon. Taste and add another lemon if you prefer a more zesty flavour.
- When you are happy with the mix, carefully spoon this over the strawberries.
- In a plastic jug or bowl, add the biscuits. Using the end of a wooden rolling pin, gently bash the biscuits to form biscuit crumbs. (You could use a food processor but I find this saves washing up!)
- Sprinkle over the biscuit crumbs and follow this with a sprinkle of brown sugar.
- Place in the fridge for at least 30 minutes until you are ready to eat.
- Preheat the halogen oven using the preheat setting or set the temperature to 250°C.
- Place the cheesecake on the high rack for 3 minutes until the top has caramelised or browned well, but not burnt. Serve when ready.

Note: As with the crème brûlèe recipe, you can use frozen or fresh strawberries. You could also try mixed summer fruit or blueberries. If you are using frozen fruit, use the defrost/thaw setting and place the fruit in an ovenproof serving dish on the low rack for 10 minutes before adding the cream cheese mixture.

SERVES 4–6

50g butter
150g sugar
Juice and zest of 2
   large or 3 medium
   lemons
4 medium eggs (or 3
   large), separated
1 teaspoon vanilla
   essence or paste
50g plain flour
300ml milk

SUITABLE FOR VEGETARIANS

Lemon Saucy Pudding

- Beat the butter and sugar together until creamy.
- Using a sharp vegetable peeler, peel the zest from 2–3 lemons (depending on desired lemony intensity). The peeler magically peels the zest and leaves the white pith behind. Finely chop the zest and add to the beaten butter/sugar mixture.
- Add the egg yolks, vanilla and lemon juice. Beat well before adding the flour and milk.
- This will form quite a runny batter. Give it a thorough stir to make sure the mixer has not left anything on the edges.
- Meanwhile, in a clean bowl, beat the egg whites until they form soft peaks. Fold into the batter gently.
- Line a baking dish with butter. I use a Pyrex baking dish but you could use individual ramekin dishes (see below). Pour in the mixture.
- Pour hot water into your halogen oven up to approximately 3cm (1inch) from the bottom. Then preheat the oven using the preheat setting or set the temperature to 150°C.
- Place the baking tray in the water to create a bain marie. If you prefer and have room, you can place a baking tray filled with water on the lower rack and add small ramekin dishes filled with the mixture.
- Cook for 40–45 minutes (20–30 minutes for individual ramekin dishes). The pudding should have a golden sponge topping which is firm to touch. When you serve the pudding, you will notice that the bottom half is a gooey lemon sauce and the top should be a lovely light sponge.
- Serve with crème fraîche or Greek yoghurt.

Butterscotch Sauce

- Place the butter, brown sugar and golden syrup in an ovenproof bowl (or saucepan if you prefer not to use the halogen oven). Melt together gently but don't let it burn. Stir well to combine.
- Fold in the double cream (must be double as single may curdle/separate).
- Serve hot or cold.

60g butter
120g brown sugar
6 tablespoons golden syrup
6 tablespoons double cream

SUITABLE FOR VEGETARIANS

Homemade Custard

- Heat the milk until just below boiling point. Meanwhile, mix the egg yolks, cornflour and sugar together. Be careful to keep an eye on the milk to avoid it spilling over.
- Remove the milk from the heat and add the egg mixture. Use a hand whisk and stir well.
- Place back on the heat and continue to stir until the custard starts to thicken – be careful not to have the heat too high or it will burn.
- Once it has reached your desired thickness remove from the heat. Serve immediately.

600ml full fat milk
4 egg yolks
4 tablespoons cornflour
3 tablespoons sugar
1 teaspoon vanilla essence

SUITABLE FOR VEGETARIANS

Note: If you have any custard left over, you could pour it into lolly moulds and freeze – these make delicious ice-lollies!

SERVES 4–6

75g butter
175g digestive biscuits,
   crushed
50g ground almonds
3 eggs, beaten
50g sugar
1 teaspoon vanilla
   essence
250g cream cheese
150g Greek yoghurt
100g blueberries
Icing sugar to sprinkle

SUITABLE FOR VEGETARIANS

Baked Blueberry Cheesecake

This is a different recipe to the Baked Raspberry Cheesecake.
Again, you can opt for different fruit if you prefer.

• Preheat the halogen oven using the preheat setting or
  set the temperature to 170°C.
• Using the heat from the preheat setting, place the
  butter in a bowl in the halogen and allow it to melt,
  but not burn. Once melted, remove from the oven
  and stir in the crushed biscuits and almonds.
• Pour this into a well greased or lined tin – I use a
  sprung-side, loose-bottomed tin for this. Press down
  firmly to form a base.
• In a food mixer, combine the eggs, sugar, vanilla,
  cream cheese and yoghurt. Once combined, stir in
  almost all of the blueberries, retaining some for
  decoration.
• Pour this mixture onto the biscuit base. Smooth out
  flat before popping onto the low rack and cooking
  for 45–50 minutes, until the cheesecake is firm and
  set. You should not have a problem, but if you feel
  the top of the cheesecake is getting too brown, you
  can cover it securely with some tin foil.
• Remove and allow to cool before decorating with the
  remaining blueberries and a sprinkle of icing sugar.

Baked Cinnamon and Hazelnut Apples

A traditional autumnal treat.

SERVES 4

- Preheat the halogen oven using the preheat setting or set the temperature to 200°C.
- Wash and core the apples, leaving the skins intact. Mix the honey with 10ml of boiling water and the cinnamon. Stir until dissolved.
- Place the apples on a baking tray or ovenproof dish and add 2 tablespoons of water to the dish. Brush the apples with the honey mixture.
- Combine the hazelnuts, sultanas and brown sugar (retaining a small amount of sugar for sprinkling). Stuff the cores of the apples with the hazelnut mixture. Finish with a sprinkling of brown sugar.
- Bake on the low rack in the halogen oven for 30–40 minutes until soft.
- Serve with low fat crème fraiche or natural yoghurt.

4 Bramley apples
2 teaspoons of runny honey
2–3 teaspoons ground cinnamon
25g chopped hazelnuts
40g sultanas
20g brown sugar
Low fat crème fraiche or natural yoghurt (optional)

SUITABLE FOR VEGETARIANS

SERVES 4–6

750g rhubarb,
   chopped
2 oranges, peeled and
   chopped
1–2 tablespoons sugar
1–2 tablespoons water
150g breadcrumbs
75g oats
2 teaspoons cinnamon
100g butter
3 tablespoons golden
   syrup

SUITABLE FOR VEGETARIANS

Orange and Rhubarb Betty

I adore rhubarb and when combined with orange this makes a wonderfully satisfying dessert. It is a great variation to the standard fruit crumble. If you fancy another variation, why not combine rhubarb and strawberries? Delicious.

- Preheat the halogen oven using the preheat setting or set the temperature to 190°C.
- Place the rhubarb and orange in an ovenproof dish. Sprinkle with the sugar and water. Place on the low rack and cook for 10 minutes. Stir to help combine flavours. Cook for another 5 minutes before removing from the oven.
- While the rhubarb is cooking, combine the breadcrumbs, oats and cinnamon. Place this mixture over the top of the fruit.
- Place the butter and syrup in an ovenproof dish and melt using the heat from the halogen oven – do not allow to burn. Once melted, pour this mixture over the crumble mixture.
- Return the dish to the halogen oven and place on the low rack. Cook for another 15–20 minutes until the top is golden.
- Serve with a dollop of crème fraîche or vanilla ice-cream.

Blueberry, Apricot and Almond Bake

SERVES 4–6

I adore this combination. When in season it is great to use fresh blueberries but, to be honest, frozen works just as well. This recipe can be prepared and cooked in minutes so it's ideal for a quick, last minute dessert when you are in need of a comforting pud!

- Place the blueberries and apricots in an ovenproof dish, making sure they are evenly spread.
- Top with a sprinkle of flaked almonds and random dollops of Greek yoghurt.
- Finish with a drizzle of runny honey to help sweeten.
- Place this on the high rack and cook at 220°C for 10 minutes.
- Serve immediately – yummy yummy!

200g blueberries
2–3 apricots, sliced (you could also use nectarines or peaches or a combination)
Handful of flaked almonds
2–3 tablespoons Greek yoghurt or crème fraîche
Drizzle of runny honey

SUITABLE FOR VEGETARIANS

SERVES 4–6

8 ripe pears, peeled,
cored and diced
2 tablespoons water
1–2 tablespoons sugar
(depending on
desired sweetness)
8–12 tablespoons
granola
75g dark chocolate
chips (if you are not
using dark chocolate
granola)
2 tablespoons
hazelnuts, chopped

Pear and Dark Chocolate Granola Layer

You can use granola and mix in your own dark chocolate chips, or try Dorset Cereals' amazing Chocolate Granolas, though I must warn you, they are seriously addictive! This pudding is lovely hot or cold.

• Place the pears in a saucepan with the water and cook until they start to soften. Once softened, stir in the sugar.
• Preheat the halogen oven using the preheat setting or set the temperature to 180°C.
• Mix the granola, chocolate chips and hazelnuts together.
• Spoon half of the pears into an ovenproof dish. Cover with a layer of granola mix. Add the final layer of pears and cover again with the granola mixture.
• Place in the oven on the low rack and cook for 15 minutes.
• Serve hot or cold.

Chocolate Saucy Pudding

My mum used to make this when we were children and I rediscovered the recipe when I pinched her personal cookery notebook. We used to call this a magic pudding as the sauce is poured over the top of the cake, but during cooking it miraculously goes to the bottom. I have adapted it to suit the halogen and it works really well. You could make it in small ramekin dishes, but adjust the cooking time.

SERVES 4–6

115g sugar
115g butter
2 eggs, beaten
2 tablespoons milk
1 tablespoon vanilla essence or paste
100g self-raising flour
2 tablespoons cocoa
300ml boiling water
2 tablespoons sugar
1 tablespoon cocoa

SUITABLE FOR VEGETARIANS

- Preheat the halogen oven using the preheat setting or set the temperature to 175°C.
- In your mixer, beat the sugar and butter together until creamy and fluffy. Gradually add the beaten eggs, milk and vanilla and mix well before adding the flour and cocoa.
- Pour into a greased ovenproof dish (or ramekin dishes) and smooth over until flat.
- In bowl or jug, mix the boiling water, sugar and cocoa together and stir thoroughly until dissolved and lump free. Pour this over the sponge mixture.
- Place on the low rack and cook for 40–50 minutes, until the sponge is firm to touch.
- Serve with a dollop of Greek yoghurt or crème fraîche and enjoy!

SERVES 4–6

6–8 slices of bread
  (ideally slightly stale)
Butter
2–3 tablespoons sugar
2–3 tablespoons dried
  fruit (currants,
  raisins and sultanas)
Zest of 1 orange
2 eggs
500ml double cream
500ml milk
Nutmeg, freshly grated

SUITABLE FOR VEGETARIANS

Bread and Butter Pudding

I blame my mum for my addiction to milky puddings. I don't drink milk so my mum used to overload me with milky puddings as a child in the belief that she was ensuring I had enough calcium in my diet. This is one of my favourites – comforting and filling, perfect for a winter's evening or when you are in need of a cuddle.

- Butter the bread – on one side or both if you prefer, and line a greased ovenproof dish with the first layer of bread slices.
- Sprinkle over sugar and dried fruit and then continue to layer until you have used up all the bread.
- In a jug combine the orange zest, eggs, cream and milk. Pour this over the bread mixture. Leave to settle for 30 minutes.
- Preheat the halogen oven using the preheat setting or set the temperature to 180°C.
- Sprinkle the top of the bread and butter pudding with freshly grated nutmeg.
- Place the pudding on the low rack and cook for 20–30 minutes until golden and set.
- Serve immediately with a dollop of cream, crème fraîche or yoghurt.

Gooey Chocolate Puddings

SERVES 4–6

These are baked in little ramekin dishes and turned out immediately – they will droop and ooze out chocolate when punctured with a spoon, but that is the general appeal. Serve with a dollop of crème fraîche and a few fresh raspberries for the perfect indulgent pud!

350g dark chocolate
60g butter
150g sugar
4 eggs
1 teaspoon vanilla extract
1 teaspoon chocolate extract (optional)
60g plain flour, sifted

SUITABLE FOR VEGETARIANS

- Melt the chocolate using a bain marie or a bowl over a saucepan of hot water (don't let the bottom of the bowl touch the water). Once melted, leave to one side.
- Meanwhile, combine the butter and sugar until light and fluffy. Add the eggs, vanilla and chocolate extract. Combine well before folding in the sifted flour.
- Finally add the chocolate and combine well.
- Preheat the halogen oven using the preheat setting or set the temperature to 200°C.
- Thoroughly grease and dust with flour 4–6 ramekin dishes. Pour in the mixture and place on the low rack.
- Cook for 12–15 minutes.
- Turn onto a serving plate, sprinkle with icing sugar and serve with a dollop of crème fraîche and some fresh raspberries – delicious!

Index